# An Atlas of English Dialects

# An Atlas
# of English
# Dialects

Clive Upton and
J. D. A. Widdowson

OXFORD UNIVERSITY PRESS

Oxford University Press, Great Clarendon Street, Oxford OX2 6DP

Oxford New York
Athens Auckland Bangkok Bogota Bombay
Buenos Aires Calcutta Cape Town Dar es Salaam
Delhi Florence Hong Kong Istanbul Karachi
Kuala Lumpur Madras Madrid Melbourne
Mexico City Nairobi Paris Singapore
Taipei Tokyo Toronto

and associated companies in
Berlin Ibadan

Oxford is a trade mark of Oxford University Press

Published in the United States by
Oxford University Press Inc., New York

British Library Cataloguing in Publication Data
Data available

Library of Congress Cataloging in Publication Data
Upton, Clive, 1946-
An atlas of English dialects/Clive Upton and J. D. A. Widdowson.
Includes bibliographical references and indexes.
1. English language—Dialects—England—Maps.
I. Widdowson, J. D. A. (John David Allison)  II. Title.
PE1705.U68  1996  427'.0022'3–dc20  95-33736
ISBN 0-19-869274-9

10 9 8 7 6 5 4

Printed in Great Britain by
Mackays of Chatham plc
Chatham, Kent

for

Stanley Ellis & Peter Wright

# CONTENTS

Acknowledgements       viii

Introduction       ix

Key to Pronunciation       xx

County Boundaries pre-1974       xxii

County Boundaries in 1996       xxiii

**THE MAPS AND COMMENTARIES    1**

Bibliography       183

Index of Maps       186

Index of Linguistic Terms       187

General Index       189

# ACKNOWLEDGEMENTS

Stewart Sanderson was our co-author on *Word Maps*, from which the *Atlas* has developed. Simon Redfern and Alan Russell undertook the lengthy preliminary listing and ordering of words for the General Index. Most notably, Edmund Weiner of Oxford University Press made innumerable vital suggestions concerning our map commentaries. This atlas could not have appeared as it does without their help. We are happy to share with them the credit for any merits which the book may have, whilst reserving the blame for any deficiencies entirely to ourselves.

C. U.
J. D. A. W.

*The Centre for English Cultural Tradition and Language*
*University of Sheffield*
MAY 1995

# INTRODUCTION

## Dialect Study and the Survey of English Dialects

> There can be no doubt that pure dialect speech is rapidly disappearing even in country districts, owing to the spread of education, and to modern facilities of intercommunication. The writing of this grammar was begun none too soon, for had it been delayed another twenty years I believe it would by then be quite impossible to get together sufficient pure dialect material to enable any one to give even a mere outline of the phonology [pronunciation] of our dialects as they existed at the close of the nineteenth century.

This was written by Joseph Wright in the Preface to *The English Dialect Grammar*, which was part of the six-volume *English Dialect Dictionary* that he published between 1898 and 1905. Although it should not be inferred from this comment that he believed the dialects which were changing in his day had until that point remained unchanged from those which had existed in former times, Wright is making an important point. Improved communications and increasing social mobility were causing an *acceleration* in the pace of dialectal change at the time in which he was writing, with the result that many ancient speech forms were disappearing from even the most conservative, isolated rural areas. Consequently the collecting and analysis upon which Wright was engaged has proved invaluable to students of English linguistic history, and it could not be replicated today.

But there is also in Wright's comment a suggestion that English dialect study beyond the 1920s would be a less rewarding occupation than it had been for Wright himself. That this has not proved to be so is demonstrated by the many studies of language variety which have been and are being carried out by individuals and institutions. The subject which Wright did so much to make popular and academically 'respectable' now has followers studying, for example, 'traditional' regional dialects such as those which are the subject of this book, the dialects of the cities, the dialects of ethnic minorities, occupational dialects, and the relationships between dialect and social class or gender.

The Survey of English Dialects, from the findings of which the maps in this book have been produced, was the earliest of what may be thought of as the modern dialect enquiries. It provides a link between older and more recent types of investigation, since its subject matter is the traditional, essentially rural dialects examined by Wright, but its research method was based on careful selection of localities and informants and the use of a questionnaire, phonetic notation, and tape-recorders. The Survey, the principal publications of which are included in the Bibliography to this volume, was the idea of the Englishman Harold Orton and the Swiss Eugen Dieth. Based at the University of Leeds, fieldworkers collected information in 313 mainly rural localities in England between 1948 and 1961. The dialect speakers sought were elderly, locally born people with little formal education, the aim being to record speech that was not greatly influenced by outside social pressures or by radio and television and other developments in communication. This aim reflects the special interest of Orton and Dieth in the history of English, an interest which they shared with Wright. In creating the first, and to date the fullest, systematically collected body of dialect material for all the English regions, Orton and his collaborators added greatly to historical linguistic studies, and they also provided data for linguistic enquiries of kinds undreamt of when they began their work.

## A Language of Dialects

British English has always been, and continues to be, a language of dialects. Wherever one goes in England, or elsewhere in Britain, there are very obvious differences between the ways in which people speak in different places. It is so with the words used, with the grammar or the way in which words are organized, and very noticeably with pronunciation or accent. Everyone in the country seems to be aware of this variety to some extent, and most of us take this diversity for granted much of the time. Paradoxically, variation in dialect, and especially in pronunciation, is a subject about which most people when pressed, and many people without requiring any invitation, are quite prepared to express an opinion. Stop anyone in the street and ask what their word is, for example, for the soft shoe that is worn when playing sports, or what their opinion is of a Geordie or a Brummie or a Cockney accent, and you can almost guarantee an interested and an interesting response. Listen to radio or television, or read the newspapers, and you will not have to wait very long before a letter is broadcast or printed, probably signed 'Disgusted', about an accent or a pronunciation or a remarkable grammatical construction.

The rich variety of dialects in England, of which we are all aware, can in large measure be attributed to the simple fact that English has been spoken in the country for upwards of 1,500 years. Even in North America, where English has been in use for some 400 years, there has been insufficient time for fragmentation of the language to occur on the scale to which it has occurred in England, although many regional varieties have transplanted to the New World. Yet it is not the time-scale alone that has resulted in such a wealth of dialect. Language, like culture, is always changing, becoming the property of succeeding generations who alter it to suit their own purposes. To understand the dialect situation in this country we must look not only at the *number* of years that the language has existed here but also at what has taken place with regard to the language *during* those years. Forces may have acted, and indeed have acted, to suppress the trend towards dialectal development. That these forces were weaker than the forces working for the growth of dialect is an important feature of the history of the language at various stages of its evolution.

English was brought to Britain by Germanic invaders usually called Anglo-Saxons. The language itself, as spoken by these people after they arrived in Britain, is sometimes called Anglo-Saxon but nowadays more usually Old English. It was a member of the West Germanic family of languages, and in the form in which it was brought to Britain it was spoken, doubtless with many local variations, over wide areas of north-west Europe at the close of the Roman period.

Attacks by Anglo-Saxon raiders were under way before the Romans left Britain around AD 410: a late Roman military title for the commander whose task it was to guard the south-east coast was 'Count of the Saxon Shore'. When the Roman garrison was withdrawn from Britain, however, Anglo-Saxon raids and settlement inevitably increased. This was the age of Hengist and Horsa, reputedly recruited as mercenaries to fight the Picts from Scotland. Invited or not, the Germanic newcomers became increasingly assertive from around AD 450 onwards. The native Britons, called *wealas*, 'foreigners' or 'Welsh' by the Anglo-Saxons, were eventually absorbed or driven to the west.

The encroachment of the Germanic invaders on Britain was not a rapid operation, nor were the invasions carried out on a particularly large scale. Small war bands, invited or uninvited, came to fight and passed the word back that the land was good. For several generations settlers spread out over the land from the south and east, in much the same way as American pioneers settled North America more than a thousand years later. They suffered checks—several apparently at the hands of a Romano-British warlord called Arthur—but eventually they came to dominate that land we now call England, together with part of southern Scotland.

To picture an Anglo-Saxon community in England around AD 500 is to see a small group of armed farming families, perhaps separated from other similar settlements by many miles of forest or fenland. All or most of the inhabitants of one community would be drawn from one small area of the north-west European seaboard. Linguistic and other social characteristics would be local, and there would be strong pressure to conform. Even when, in the course of time, powerful leaders established themselves as kings, their territories were at first very small, and for much of the Anglo-Saxon period England was divided into a minimum of seven kingdoms. Anything approaching a truly national identity only emerged in the ninth century.

Furthermore, it appears that it was not only the history of the Anglo-Saxons after they had settled in England that encouraged the development of local idiosyncrasies. The Anglo-Saxon historian Bede claimed that the Germanic invaders were drawn from three distinct peoples, the Angles, Saxons, and Jutes. The Jutes, early settlers in Kent from where they colonized the Isle of Wight and part of Hampshire, may have come from Jutland, although there is little evidence for this. The Angles probably came largely from southern Denmark, from an area that became known as Angeln, and settled in the eastern parts of the country as far north as south-east Scotland and throughout the English Midlands. But whereas the Jutes and Angles probably had as their core a tribal unit, the Saxons were a much more loosely knit group. Taking, or being given, their name from the *seax*, the single-bladed long-knife that was one of their favourite weapons, they were raiders from anywhere along the coastal lands from what is now northern Germany to northern France. These raiders settled in the largest numbers in the south and south-west of Britain. Such a loose confederation of war bands would have brought with them a multiplicity of customs, traditions, and dialects. Also, they may be expected to hold together only as long as unity was needed against a common enemy. And indeed, once they were established in 'England', the Saxons, and the Angles and Jutes too, proved to be as ready to fight each other as to fight the Britons.

A final important factor working against any tendency towards uniformity of language, at least for the first two centuries of Anglo-Saxon settlement, was that most people, from the king downwards, were illiterate. The Christian missionary Augustine arrived in southern England in AD 597, and the influence of Columba reached the north a little later. With Christianity and 'education' some pressure for conformity to a standard form of language, at least within individual kingdoms, came to be felt by those who could write: it is the experience of most of us that we write in a much more conformist way than we speak. By the time this pressure developed, however, English was well established in the country in a wealth of spoken forms, and most people can have had little cause or opportunity to write it anyway.

The legacy bequeathed to English by those who brought it into England was, therefore, one of variety. There was little need for the Anglo-Saxons to invent or conform to a widespread standard and, doubtless, for many people there was every inclination to promote their own local brand.

Then came the Vikings. Beginning in about AD 800, raids rapidly increased in size, intensity, and duration, until by the 860s Viking armies were staying in England for several years at a time. By the late ninth century Scandinavian settlements were being established in the north and east, and the Vikings were transformed from raiders into conquerors controlling roughly half the land of England.

The Viking invasions created some pressure towards standardization of English. Most of the northern kingdom of Northumbria was overrun, and so too was the eastern part of the Midland kingdom of Mercia. English resistance to the Vikings, and the survival of English tradition and language, came to be centred on Alfred's kingdom of Wessex. Then, with

Alfred's victory over Guthrum in AD 878, the relationship between the two peoples was in large measure stabilized. The 'Danelaw' was established for the Vikings north and east of a line running roughly from London to Chester; Wessex, with West Mercia also under Alfred's control, was secure. The culture and language of Wessex became synonymous with English culture and language for those for whom learning was significant.

Yet although the permanent settlement of Vikings in England forced a measure of uniformity on the English language, it also introduced further variety. The language spoken by the Vikings, today called Old Norse, was, like English, a Germanic language. Limited communication may have taken place between Anglo-Saxons and Vikings using their own languages, especially if the former used an Anglian form of English. At first pure Norse would have been spoken in the Scandinavian settlements in England, no doubt with Danish, Norwegian, Swedish, Icelandic, and more localized variations. In time, however, the 'English' Vikings adopted an English identity. Their language assumed an increasingly English character whilst retaining strong Norse features, elements of which can be clearly identified in the dialects and place-names of the old Danelaw today.

The upheavals of the Viking period in England had hardly subsided when a new invasion occurred. The Norman Conquest of 1066 was not quite the devastating event that it is sometimes made out to have been. Edward the Confessor was half Norman; the Normans were only four or five generations removed from Viking forbears. Cultures in Normandy and England were not entirely dissimilar, and at court level at least there was considerable contact. Nevertheless, because of the manner of their coming and the language which they brought, the Normans had a profound effect on English, not least in ensuring the continued existence and even the strengthening of dialectal variety.

The Normans, in spite of their Scandinavian ancestry, spoke French. Being Romance or Italic rather than Germanic, French was 'foreign' to English in a way that Norse had never been. There could be little contact between English and Norman unless one learnt the other's language. However, the Normans came to England not as settlers, to mingle with the native population, but as a master race, to rule and to exploit. For some generations they had little interest in learning the native language, and only a few gifted or privileged English men and women acquired Norman French, usually as members of Norman households or in the service of the Norman administration. French was the language of a small élite. English was the language of the village and the workplace, used by the majority, the ordinary and largely unlettered people. As such it was a spoken language, used, as early Old English had been, within restricted geographical areas for everyday communication. It had little need to be anything other than homely and local. And if regional diversity helped to obscure it and to inhibit its mastery by aliens, one suspects that the popular opinion was 'so much the better!'

Slowly, with the weakening of ties with Normandy and France, English came to be rehabilitated as the national language. In 1362, at a time of nationalistic fervour and of particular antagonism towards France, the king's speech at the opening of parliament was in English for the first time, and in the same year business in the law courts began to be carried out in English too. In the later part of the fourteenth century Chaucer in an East Midland dialect, Langland in a South-west Midland dialect, and the 'Gawain Poet' in the North-west Midlands were in the forefront of a flowering of vernacular literature, in which English was married to borrowed French vocabulary and artistic forms. English was clearly finding favour in high places.

Through such influences as those of Chaucer, the universities of Oxford and Cambridge, and London with its court and large population, an East Midland variety of English came to be regarded as the written standard. The establishment of this standard took a long time, and at first it only applied to English written for widespread consumption. At the heart of the royal court in the late sixteenth century, Sir Walter Raleigh is reputed to have retained his Devon speech, though his written English was not especially regional. As evidence that pressure was on to standardize the written language whilst recognizing that even upper-class speech could be non-standard, we have only to cite the following, written in 1589 in a handbook on the art of the poet, *The Arte of English Poesie*:

neither shall he take termes of Northernmen, such as they vse in dayly talke, whether they be noble men or gentlemen, or of their best clerkes all is a matter: nor in effect any speach vsed beyond the river of Trent, though no man can deny but that theirs is the purer English Saxon at this day, yet it is not so Courtly nor yet so currant as our Southerne English is, no more is the far Westerne mans speach: ye shall therfore take the vsuall speach of the Court, and that of London and the shires lying about London within xl myles, and not much above.

From this point onwards the way for non-standard dialectal English was downwards in the estimation of the arbiters of fashion. The Restoration squire was ridiculed for his local speech as for his provincial manners. Ridicule turned increasingly to distaste in the eighteenth century, as influential intellectuals such as Swift, Dryden, and Johnson argued for the imposing or 'fixing' of a standard language, and grammar writers strove to describe English according to the Latin model. Increasing democratization of society in the nineteenth century, together with improved communications, began the slow process of exposing everyone to the rich variety of regional dialects existing in the country. On the other hand, the same developments spread the powerful influence of the standard form of the language, and progress in education, in the professions, and in society continued to depend on the possession of an acceptable accent and a grasp of the 'correct' grammar and vocabulary. In the course of time the British Broadcasting Corporation would come to select its announcers and newsreaders on considerations of accent which went far beyond the dictates of intelligibility. Yet with their roots firmly fixed in the history of the language, the dialects of England have persisted through the generations. Whatever was useful in each new age has been added to local speech as well as to the standard 'supra-dialect': Scandinavian and French words through invasion; Classical and Romance words in the Renaissance; words from many other languages through colonization and trade; continuous changes in pronunciation. Nevertheless, the diversity of accent, vocabulary, and grammar could not be levelled by forces which had little meaning for the vast majority of English people, as today's vigorous dialects show. Such levelling as there has been is most evident in standardization of grammar and in erosion of obsolescent sections of vocabulary including, for example, many variants of older agricultural terms. This is, however, simply part of a continuing process of change which has left regional speech, and especially regional accents, relatively unscathed.

## Using the *Atlas*

The maps in this atlas are based on those of an earlier work interpreting the findings of the Survey of English Dialects, *Word Maps*, which was published in 1987, although they have been redrawn to take account of boundary changes which have recently taken place and, in some cases, in order to satisfy the demands of the commentaries which accompany each map here and which were not present in the earlier work. A map showing the names of all the counties is given on page xxiii. Also, since the SED records refer to the old, pre-1974 counties, a map is provided on page xxii which shows the earlier boundaries and county names.

The ninety maps are arranged in a broadly thematic manner. However, the logic of this ordering is not strictly adhered to when it is felt that another arrangement is preferable in order that some special point may be made. Furthermore, some maps can be considered to fit one of the identified themes only very loosely. The general ordering of maps is as follows: Pronunciation (vowels, then consonants, Maps 1 to 25); Grammar (Maps 26 to 35); People (Maps 36 to 40); the Body (Maps 41 to 44); States and Conditions (Maps 45 to 58); Animals (Maps 59 to 65); Nature (Maps 66 to 70); Objects (Maps 71 to 74); Seasons and Times (Maps 75 to 78); Actions (Maps 79 to 90).

Although each map can be considered to be essentially concerned with pronunciation (Maps 1 to 25), grammar (Maps 26 to 35), or vocabulary (Maps 36 to 90), the commentaries which accompany each may be expected to discuss anything of linguistic interest concerning the information shown. The maps which have underlined letters in their titles, and on which information is written in small, lower-case, lettering, are concerned with variation in pronunciation: the underlined letters in the titles are those for which dialectal pronunciations are given. Instead of using phonetic script to indicate pronunciations, we have used the ordinary letters of the alphabet in what is technically known as a respelling system, and a Key to Pronunciation is provided. The remainder of the maps show their grammatical and vocabulary information in capital, UPPER CASE, lettering.

The commentaries for each map make use of the same lettering conventions as the maps: SMALL CAPITALS for words, **lower case** (in **bold** type, in order that it may be readily seen) for pronunciations. *Italic* type is used to identify historical forms of words, words of particular interest which are not central to the commentary, and letters used in spellings (to identify the letter *a*, the letter *b* and so on). *Italics* are also used conventionally in references to books cited, and to indicate emphasis. When a markedly linguistic term is used in the commentaries, this is given in ***bold italics*** in that commentary which is judged to hold the most helpful explanation of its meaning: an Index of Linguistic Terms which refers to these commentaries is given towards the end of the book.

The different dialect areas on a map are delineated by lines called *isoglosses*. These are drawn to run midway between localities which were discovered by the SED to use the different pronunciations or words which are the subject of the map. Each map reveals areas in which particular words or pronunciations are concentrated, with the areas shading into one another rather than being sharply demarcated, and it should be borne in mind that the labels are those for the forms which were found to be *dominant* in the various regions. Sometimes a locality within an area was found to have a different usage, or one locality exhibited both the form used throughout the surrounding area and another, less usual, form. Such occurrences have not been included in the *Atlas*, although all the information is of course available in various other publications based on the Survey. There have also been occasions when, in order to avoid creating a larger number of areas than can comfortably be included on a small-scale map, similar forms have been grouped together as one. A good example of this is in the AUTUMN map, where the minor variations *fall of the leaf* and *fall of the year* are regarded as examples of FALL.

Non-standard dialects are, of course, essentially spoken, and the spelling of dialect words sometimes presents problems. It is good policy to spell words as they sound wherever possible, and this policy has been followed here. However, there are some words in this atlas which have been spelt in the *Oxford English Dictionary* or the *English Dialect Dictionary* in ways which reflect their history as written words. Since it is expected that readers may wish to look up words there, those dictionaries' spellings are used unless they are likely to be particularly misleading. So, although *nieve*, 'fist', could helpfully be written NEEV, the dictionary form NIEVE is used as it is unlikely to cause a reader great difficulty.

It should be remembered that the maps are concerned with England, including the Isle of Man and, for reasons still prevailing when the SED was undertaken, Gwent (formerly Monmouthshire) in south-east Wales. The isoglosses indicating dialect boundaries on the maps therefore stop at the Scottish and Welsh (and Gwent–Glamorgan) borders. When, for reasons of space, a label has been written across a national boundary, it must only be taken to be relevant for that area of England and Gwent to which it is attached. The Isle of Man is usually given its own label detailing the forms recorded there, although since only two localities were studied on the island it is left unlabelled if those localities produced different forms.

The dialect areas shown on the maps are, as we have said, based on generalizations, and the labels within them only refer to dominant dialectal forms. It should not be inferred from the maps that forms other than those labelled for a region are never used dialectally in that region. Also, isoglosses are never firm boundaries restricting the movement of dialectal forms from place to place. The boundary lines are always moving: some may even disappear completely and new ones may appear while collectors record their information and analyse it. Our language is changing all the time, and we hope that readers will wish to test this for themselves, using the maps in this book as a starting-point for their own investigations.

# KEY TO PRONUNCIATION

The system for indicating pronunciation on the pronunciation maps is simple. It is based as closely as possible on common sounds of the ordinary letters of the English alphabet. In almost all cases you will reproduce the sounds accurately if you read them aloud as they are written.

For guidance, notes are given below on the representation of vowel-sounds, and of consonants for which some special comment is necessary.

## The Vowel System

The basic building blocks are the five English vowels, **a**, **e**, **i**, **o**, and **u**. In the maps these are sometimes used alone, sometimes doubled, and sometimes combined with other vowels or with consonants to indicate more complex sounds. Looking at each vowel in turn, together with other sounds that can be grouped with them, there are five groups:

- the **a** group
  - **a**      as in *man*
  - **aa**     the sound in *man*, made longer
  - **ah**     the sound in *far*, without sounding the *r*
  - **aw**     as in *draw*
  - **ay**     as in *day*
  - **a-i**    the **a** in *man* plus the **i** in *pin* (a form of the vowel-sound of *time* in southern British English)
  - **ah-i**   the **ah**-sound in *far* plus the **i** in *pin*

- the **e** group
  - **e**      as in *pen*
  - **ee**     as in *been*

- the **i** group
  - **i**      as in *pin*
  - **i-uh**   the **i** in *pin* plus the **uh**-sound in *fun*

- the **o** group
  **o**　　as in *hot*
  **oo**　　short, the sound in *put*
  **oo**　　long, as in *moon*
  **ow**　　as in *show*
  **oy**　　as in *boy*

- the **u** group
  **uh**　　the sound in *fun* in southern British English
  **uh-i**　the **uh**-sound in *fun* plus the **i** in *pin*

## The Consonant System

Most letters need no explanation: simply say them in an everyday British English accent. The following need some comment:

**dh**　　the 'hard' *th*-sound in *this* (*th* has been used exclusively for the 'soft' *th*-sound, as in *thin*)

**ngg**　the ordinary *ng*-sound as in *ring* plus an additional 'hard' *g*-sound

**zh**　　the sound of the second *g* in *garage*, using the 'softer', non-*j* pronunciation

# COUNTY BOUNDARIES PRE-1974

The county boundaries to 1974, as used in the Survey of English Dialects.

# COUNTY BOUNDARIES IN 1996

The county boundaries in 1996, as used in this Atlas.

# Maps and Commentaries

**B<u>U</u>RIED**

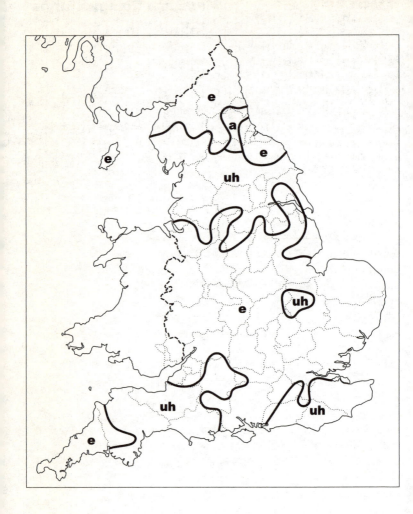

2

MAP 1

# B<u>U</u>RIED

*Old English*, the English of the period from approximately AD 450 to 1100, had as its form of TO BURY *byrgan*, in which the letter *g* had a **y** pronunciation and, more importantly for this map, the letter *y* had a special short **oo** sound close to a 'French *u*'. According to Joseph and Elizabeth Wright (*Middle English Grammar*, para. 49), the change of this sound to **e** is one which first took place in Kent and the surrounding areas late in the Old English period. For a small number of words which had been spelt with *y* in Old English this Kentish pronunciation eventually found its way into *Standard English*, the generally accepted varieties of English which are comparatively free from obviously localized speech-forms. It was usually signalled too by an *e* appearing in the spelling, giving for example KNELL from Old English *cnyll* and MERRY from Old English *myrige*.

This change of a variety of short **oo** to **e** was not the normal one for those words which were spelt with *y* in Old English. The most common development for the sound has been to **i**. Most words which had a *y* spelling underwent this change during the *Middle English* period, that is between approximately AD 1100 and 1500, resulting in such modern *i*-spelt words as BRIDGE, KISS, LISTEN, and SISTER. However, as a further complicating factor, especially in the West Midlands the Old English **oo**-type pronunciation lived on beyond the Middle English period, later changing only slightly. This pronunciation too has had an influence on Standard English, resulting in Old English *y* words such as BLUSH, MUCH, CHURCH, now spelt with *u* and with **uh** or **er** pronunciations.

BURIED thus shows the influence of two strands in the development of the Old English *y* short **oo**-sound. Its standard pronunciation, **e**, shows the Kentish development, and this pronunciation is seen to exist in the non-standard dialects of the far North, Midland, Southern, and far South-western England. However **uh**, still signalled by its spelling, is seen to persist in an area which, in southern Lancashire and South and West Yorkshire, contains part of the historical West Midland speech area. It is remarkable that it also remains firmly established in south-eastern areas where standard **e** began.

The northern **a** area is attested by Wright in his *Dialect Grammar*.

MAP 2

# HAND

Although **a** is the original Old English vowel sound in HAND, the existence of an **o** pronunciation is itself very ancient. To quote Trudgill, *Dialects of England*, 23: "In Anglo-Saxon times there developed a strong tendency in certain areas of England to change a short 'a' to a short 'o' in words where the vowel occurred in front of an <u>n</u>. Thus 'land' became 'lond' just as 'lang' became 'long'. However, this change was much less successful than the 'lang' to 'long' change, and took root only in western areas of the country." This both summarizes and simplifies a complicated situation which in many dialects involved the introduction of long vowel-sounds for a time in the late Old English and early Middle English periods before a short sound again became the norm. The **o** area for HAND is contracting, but the sound remains characteristic of the pronunciation of many West Midlanders more than a thousand years after it was first heard in such words as HAND and LAND. Joseph and Elizabeth Wright point out in their *New English Grammar* (para. 63) that in at least one case the old **a/o** variation has usefully survived into standard Modern English, giving us the separate though related words BAND and BOND.

The **e** pronunciation found in the South-east appears to be an exaggerated form of the type of **a** which is associated with south-eastern speech and with a conservative form of the standard ***Received Pronunciation*** (or ***RP***) accent. This variety of **a**, which for simplicity can be called 'southern **a**', is best described as '*a* with a flavour of *e*'. In the ***International Phonetic Alphabet*** (***IPA***) it is transcribed as [æ], using the combined a + e symbol called 'aesc' (**ash**). To many northerners southern **a** sounds like **e**, and it is not hard to see how this kind of **a** at times slips over into the full **e** pronunciation to which it is so close.

'Ordinary' (as opposed to southern) **a** was the normal short *a* sound in English until the late sixteenth century, at which time a general trend towards southern **a** occurred. Southern **a** then remained as the standard short *a* sound until very recent times. It continues to be used by most North Americans. During the second half of the twentieth century, however, there has been a noticeable move back towards an ordinary **a** in Britain. The move from southern towards ordinary **a** is one which marks out younger from older speakers of Received Pronunciation and one which, in the words of Wells (*Accents of English*, 292) "promises to carry RP further away from both American and southern-hemisphere accents of English".

MAP 3
# LAST

Along with the distinction between northern **oo** and southern **uh** in such a word as SUN, the distinction between the use of a short vowel in the north and a long vowel in the south in such words as LAST is one which speakers of British English habitually use to locate an English person's origins by her or his accent. This map can therefore usefully be compared with that for SUN (Map 7), as it can with the map for AUNT(IE) (Map 4), where 'short' and 'long' *a* also occur, albeit with a different history from that applying to LAST.

The varieties of pronunciation with which we are concerned here apply to situations where an *a*-sound is followed not only by **s** as in LAST but also where it is followed by **f** (for example in CHAFF) or by **th** (in PATH). With only minor changes the sound remained short, as **a**, for more than a thousand years after the Anglo-Saxon invasion of England. During the seventeenth century, however, it became fashionable to lengthen this sound while still pronouncing it much as the short sound had been pronounced: Ekwall, in *English Sounds and Morphology* (para. 46), traces the first written record of the change to 1685. It is this new sound which is seen to survive as **aa** in the speech of non-standard speakers over most of the southern half of England. By the eighteenth century a further change had taken place, in which the lengthened sound came to be articulated further back in the mouth, giving **ah**: this development took root in the South-east, from where it influenced the Received Pronunciation of standard speakers around the country, but its non-standard geographical spread has remained quite restricted. This sound-change can be contrasted with that of the parallel lengthening of **o** before **s**, **f**, and **th** (Map 5).

There are two surprising non-standard pronunciations shown for LAST. One is the **ay** sound located on the border of Devon and Cornwall, which has no explanation but is similar to a pronunciation for LAST which Wright records in the *Dialect Grammar* as being found in Cornwall and Wiltshire. The other unusual sound is **aar**, which represents the southern **aa** sound followed by an **r**, a feature of rhotic accents where a written *r* is pronounced (see ARM, Map 15). Shropshire is not typically an area for rhoticity, and anyway LAST does not contain a letter *r*. It appears that a **laarst** pronunciation has arisen here through *misanalysis* of the word as one which contains an *r*.

MAP 4
# A̲U̲NT(IE)

The word for which the vowel pronunciation is mapped here is primarily AUNT, this being used throughout England. However, pronunciations of the well-known less formal word AUNTIE or AUNTY are also used, as are pronunciations of a related word NAUNT.

The sound which was spelt with *au* in ***Anglo-Norman***, that is in the French used in England after the Norman Conquest, when it was followed by an *n*, has usually become modern English **aw**, as words such as HAUNCH and DAUNT testify. However, a number of words which have or once had an *au* spelling, of which AUNT, CHANT, and DANCE are examples, were influenced by a Central French pronunciation to develop an **ah** sound in the standard form instead. There is now little sign of the **aw** pronunciation for AUNT, but the **o** area in Derbyshire and Yorkshire does appear to be a survival of this Anglo-Norman sound.

Although the **ah** in AUNT is from a different source, its distribution and that of its variants can now be seen to be somewhat similar to that of the vowels in such words as GRASS, CHAFF, and PATH. This map should therefore be compared with that for LAST (Map 3). The principal distinction is between a short sound in the north and longer sounds in the south, with the standard **ah** largely restricted to the South-east on both maps. There are, however, marked differences between the two sets of words: most noticeably, the **a** area in AUNT(IE) in the South-west is not found there in such words as LAST.

On this map the boundary between short **a** and long **aa** in Devon and Cornwall is also essentially the boundary between AUNT (Devon) and AUNTIE (Cornwall). Like ADDER (Map 59), NAUNT is created by a rearrangement of the boundaries between words, though in this case an initial **n** is gained rather than lost. As Wright explains (*Dialect Grammar*, para. 266), the initial *n* has been borrowed partly from the ***indefinite article*** AN (AN AUNT becomes A NAUNT) and partly too from the ***possessive pronoun*** MINE (MINE AUNT becomes MY NAUNT).

# CR<u>O</u>SS

MAP 5
# CR**O**SS

There is a remarkably clear-cut division of non-standard speakers north and south of the Wash, with those to the north using the short **o** pronunciation in CROSS and those to the south using the long **aw** sound. Few traditional dialect speakers use both forms or use the sound which is not typical of their area.

The original vowel sound in CROSS was **o**, which was in use both in Old English and in *Old Norse* (*ON*), the language of the Viking settlers in England in the ninth and tenth centuries. This would have been the standard sound until the seventeenth century, when a development took place in which **o** became lengthened to **aw**, the vowel sound in RP *door*, before **s**, **f**, and **th**. This led to **aw** regularly being found in such words as MOSS, COST, LOFT, OFTEN, BROTH, and MOTH. The fact that this was a development in the standard variety of the language probably accounts for the fact that **aw** remains firmly entrenched in Southern England today, this being the area with which that variety is most closely associated.

The change of **o** to **aw** was apparently a major development in standard and non-standard pronunciation but, unlike that of the parallel lengthening of **a** (Map 3), it was comparatively short-lived in the standard. Although it is still possible to hear some speakers of the RP accent using **aw** in preference to **o** in such words as CROSS, they are typically older rather than younger and are in a minority even within their age group. Standard pronunciation of all those words mentioned, and of others such as GLOSS, OFF, and CLOTH, is now much more typically with **o**. According to Joseph and Elizabeth Wright (*New English Grammar*, para. 93) the **o** pronunciation was, when they wrote in the first quarter of the twentieth century, especially common in words of more than one syllable such as GOSPEL and HOSPITAL: **aw** in such words would certainly sound strange today.

The **ah** found to the north of the Severn estuary is the result of a non-standard dialect tendency towards the lengthening of **o** in many single-syllable words, even when it is not followed by **s**, **f**, or **th**, this lengthening giving rise to a wide variety of sounds in such words as DOG and BOX. Pronunciation of CROSS and similar words with **ah**, and also with **aw**, has parallels in North American speech.

# AM<u>O</u>NG(ST)

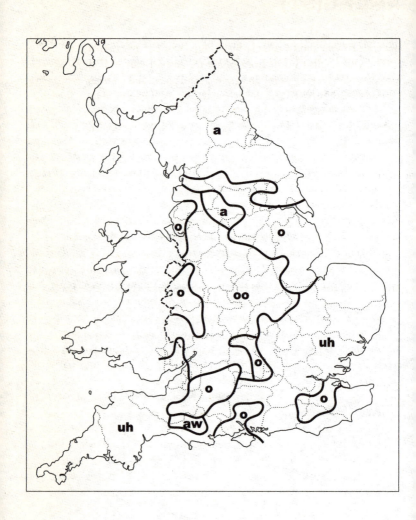

MAP 6

# AM<u>O</u>NG(ST)

**oo** represents the short *u* sound usually found in such words as FOOT.

The Old English words from which the second part of both AMONG and AMONGST derive were *gemang* and *gemong*, and both **a** and **o** pronunciations can be seen to have survived into the twentieth century. The **a** pronunciation which is found widely in Northern England is a survival of Old English *gemang*, whilst the **o**, **aw**, **oo**, and **uh** pronunciations all apparently have connections with Old English *gemong*.

The change from **o** to **oo** in AMONG and some other words with following **ng** such as MONGER and MONGREL first took place in the West Midland dialects in the Middle English period: this change accounts for the existence of a strong West Midlands **oo** area surrounded by areas of **o**. Joseph and Elizabeth Wright (*New English Grammar*, para. 139) say that from the West Midland dialects the pronunciation "crept into standard N[ew] E[nglish]".

In those areas where **oo** became **uh** in such words as BUS and MOTHER during the late sixteenth or early seventeenth century, this change naturally took place in AMONG and AMONGST too if these had the **oo** pronunciation. The commentary on SUN (Map 7), gives an explanation of this development.

It is surprising to find a small area of **aw** in Somerset and Dorset. Although this pronunciation is sometimes heard in place of **o** in words with following **s**, **f**, or **th**, such as CROSS (Map 5), OFF, or CLOTH, it is not usually associated with words in which **ng** follows the vowel.

MAP 7

# SUN

**oo** represents the short *u* sound usually found in such words as FOOT.

The use of **oo** or **uh** pronunciations in words such as SUN, BUS, and MOTHER clearly distinguishes Northern and North Midland speakers from those of the South and South Midlands, and this map can helpfully be compared with that for LAST (Map 3), where 'short' or 'long' *a* is the other north-versus-south test which English people commonly apply to accents. **oo** is the older pronunciation, being generally used in England until the late sixteenth or early seventeenth century, at which time the change to **uh** occurred in the standard and many southern dialects. The **uh** sound is markedly different from **oo**, and in its purest form sounds to many Northerners very similar to **a**. In fact comparatively few non-standard dialect speakers use this pure **uh** pronunciation, using instead a sound which, although based on **uh**, has a hint of **oo** about it. Many speakers of Received Pronunciation can now be heard to use this intermediate or *fudged sound* too.

The **o** pronunciation now located in Kent and Sussex was formerly found much more widely. Wright (*Dialect Grammar*, para. 101) records **o** in SUN in Buckinghamshire and in other similar words as far north as Cumberland and as far south as Devon. The presence of a *nasal consonant* (**n**, **m**, **ng**) before or especially after the vowel sound has historically been influential in the development of **oo** into **o**: Joseph and Elizabeth Wright (*New English Grammar*, para. 48) record many Middle English spellings with *o* for such words as HUNGER and HUNTER, suggesting that an **o** pronunciation was once to be heard in such words. However, *u* was normally written as *v* in Middle English, and the whole matter is complicated by the frequent writing of *o* for this *v* (*u*) next to such angular consonants as *n*, *m*, and *w* to make them easier to read.

**i**, found in Devon and Cornwall, is recorded in the *Dialect Grammar* (para. 100) as being used in Somerset and Devon. This pronunciation appears to have receded westwards during the first half of the twentieth century, the period between Wright's study and that of the Survey of English Dialects. It is not surprising to find RP **uh** in the extreme South-west, where English was established comparatively late. (On this phenomenon see the commentary for FIND, Map 9.)

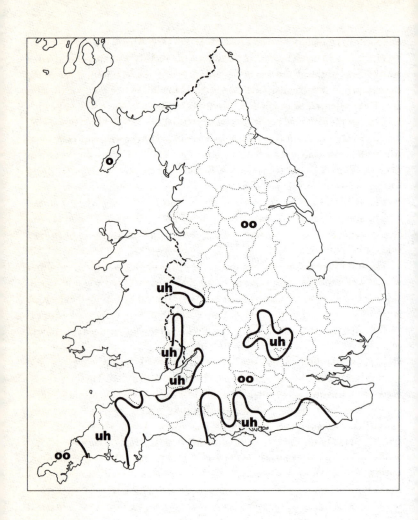

MAP 8
# to PUT

PUT is one of two sets of words which, unlike SUN (Map 7), did not see a development of Middle English short **oo** to Modern English **uh**. Both sets of words begin with a *labial* sound, that is a sound such as **p**, **b**, or **w** which is produced by closing or nearly closing the lips. One of the sets has an initial labial, then the *u*-vowel, then **l**; the other set has an initial labial and the *u*-vowel, but no following **l**.

The first set of words, those with labial consonant + vowel + **l**, includes English-derived words such as BULL, BULLOCK, FULL, PULL, WOLF, and WOOL, and French-derived words such as BULLET, BULLION, PULLET, and PULPIT. These have all generally kept their short **oo** pronunciations in Modern English, never having undergone the sixteenth and seventeenth century change of **oo** to **uh**.

The second set of words, those with labial consonant + vowel but without following **l**, includes PUT and also BUSH, BUSHEL, BUTCHER, PUDDING, PUSH, PUSS, WOMAN, and WOOD. When many words such as SUN were exchanging their Middle English short **oo** for Modern English **uh**, words in this set were also to be heard with either pronunciation. However, in the eighteenth century their standard pronunciation became fixed on the older **oo** sound, although clearly **uh** is still to be found in non-standard speech in the South and West and is the sound used in the golfing word PUTT, a variant of the ordinary PUT.

A force likely to influence some speakers to use **uh** in such a word as PUT is *hypercorrection*, which is a tendency to avoid a form believed to be non-standard (and in the speaker's view therefore inferior) when in fact it is standard. The speaker, aware that the standard vowel in SUN is **uh** rather than short **oo**, incorrectly avoids the **oo** sound in those places where a standard speaker normally uses it, saying, for example, **buhcher** and **puhdding**. It is also possible to account for the tendency of some speakers to pronounce WANT as **wuhnt** in terms of hypercorrection: the speaker knows that the standard pronunciation of ONE is **wuhn** rather than **won**, and therefore says **wuhnt** rather than standard **wont** by analogy.

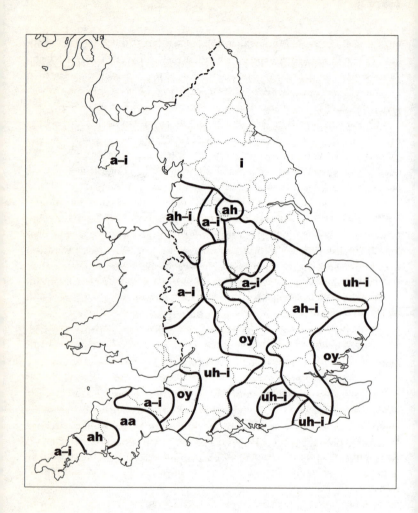

MAP 9
# FIND

The short **i** sound which is seen to be strongly supported in Northern England was used in this word in the Old English period. It can be regarded as the ancestor of all the later pronunciations. The location of this sound in the non-standard dialects as recorded in SED is little changed from that recorded by Wright (*Dialect Grammar*, para. 75).

During the late Old English period the short sound changed in Standard English, at first becoming long **ee** and then changing to **uh-i** in Middle English. The modern standard sound **a-i** developed from this during the seventeenth century. The sequence of development of the standard sound was therefore

OE **i** → late OE **ee** → ME **uh-i** → RP **a-i**

(Dobson, *English Pronunciation 1500–1700*, para. 137.) The change from a single vowel or *monophthong* to a *diphthong* made up of two vowel-sounds is known as *breaking* or *fracture*.

It is interesting to see that today's RP sound **a-i** is not widely used in the non-standard dialects, being largely confined to small areas in the Midlands and the South-west. With the exception of the large **i** area already referred to and a small **ah** area in South and West Yorkshire, Devon and Cornwall, all pronunciations are diphthongs, but except for RP **a-i** they start with sounds that are made well back in the mouth (**ah**, **uh**, **o**), resulting in pronunciations that are very different from the standard.

It is not unusual to see noticeably standard forms of pronunciation in the extreme South-west of England. During the Middle English period when the English non-standard dialects were developing, English was not much spoken in this area, where Cornish, a Celtic language closely related to Welsh, was the everyday language of most people. However, the numbers of Cornish speakers declined sharply from the sixteenth century onwards as Cornwall came to be increasingly dominated by government from London. During the long, slow decline of Cornish it was the standard forms of English pronunciation that tended to be learnt in Cornwall, just as foreign learners of English nowadays learn today's RP pronunciations. SUN and FINGER (Maps 7 and 20), show the same feature.

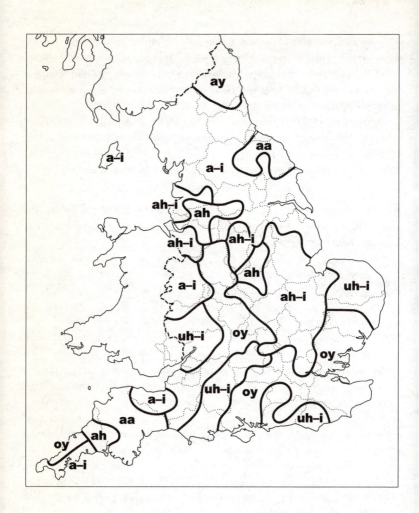

MAP 10
# FI̲VE

It is interesting to compare this map with that for FIND (Map 9). The vowel-sound of the standard pronunciation of both FIND and FIVE is the diphthong **a-i**. In both words several of the non-standard pronunciations are diphthongs too: **ah-i, oy, uh-i**, whilst others are the long monophthongal sounds **aa** and **ah**. The distribution of all these sounds is approximately the same for both words: standard diphthongs in parts of the West Midlands and South-west, other diphthongs in the Midlands and South-east, long sounds in the North Midlands and the South-west.

The real difference between the two maps is quite obviously in the sounds shown for Northern England. Here the map for FIND shows the simple short **i** sound extending over virtually the whole of the North and the north-east Midlands. As the FIND map commentary explains, this sound is a survival of the Old English original. Short **i** is, however, entirely missing from the FIVE map, the Northern and north-east Midland area being occupied by two sounds, **a-i** and **aa**, which are found elsewhere also, and another, **ay**, which is unique to the extreme North-east.

Absence of any evidence of an **i** pronunciation in FIVE, while it is well attested in FIND, immediately suggests that, in spite of the similarity in pronunciation of the two words in modern standard and non-standard speech, they have somewhat different histories. This is in fact the case. As we have seen, the Old English form of FIND had the vowel **i** which still exists as a Northern pronunciation, this short sound later becoming long **ee**. However, Old English FIVE did not have **i**, but already had the long vowel sound, **ee**, at the earliest stage of its history. From the Middle English period onwards both words, possessing an **ee** pronunciation, developed generally similar standard and non-standard varieties. Only FIND, however, has the **i**, which it had in its earliest form.

# SH<u>EE</u>P

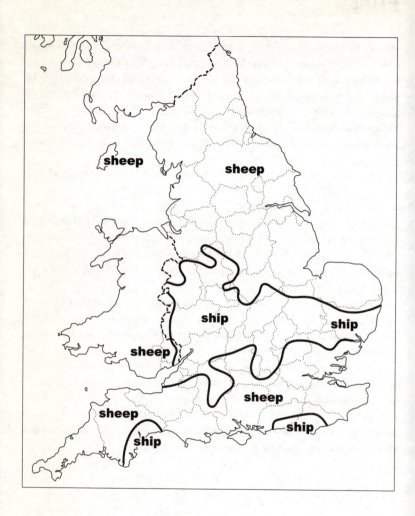

MAP 11

# SHEEP

During the Middle English period the vowel-sound in SHEEP was 'long close *e*', which in IPA phonetics is transcribed [e:]. This sound is something like the **e** we have in MET (**met**), but in phonetic terms it is both longer and *closer* (that is, pronounced with the tongue a bit higher in the mouth) than that precise sound. The length is indicated by the doubling of the letter *e* in the spelling as we have it now. This long **e** was the vowel sound of that time for many words which, like SHEEP, are now pronounced with **ee**, for example HE, ME, WE, BE, FIELD, STEEL, STREET, and WEAK. Towards the end of the Middle English period, in the late fifteenth century, the regular development of the sound was to the **ee** which is typically heard today.

However, a common feature of the development of Middle English was that long vowels came frequently to be pronounced short, especially in *monosyllables*, that is words of only one syllable. Very late in the Middle English period therefore, after words which had previously been pronounced with the long **e** had come to be pronounced with **ee**, there was a tendency for such words to have the **ee** shortened to **i** (Wright, *New English Grammar*, para. 95; Dobson, *English Pronunciation 1500–1700*, para 31). This process was quite random: as Joseph and Elizabeth Wright say, "It is almost impossible to lay down any hard and fast rules about the shortening of long vowels in N[ew]E[nglish]… In early NE the long and the shortened vowels often existed side by side in the same words, and then later one or the other became standardized." The shortened form has given us the modern standard pronunciations of such words as GRIT and SIEVE which for much of the Middle English period had pronunciations with the long **e**. It also accounts for the pronunciation of GREENWICH as **grinij** or **grenij** when GREEN is pronounced **green**, for the two pronunciations **britches** and **breetches** for BREECHES 'trousers', and for the existence of the non-standard pronunciation **ship** for SHEEP.

It is a matter of debate whether the word SHIP in 'to spoil the ship for a ha'porth of tar' refers to a boat or a sheep: tar is used in keeping boats seaworthy and was formerly used in treating sores on sheep. The debate cannot be resolved on linguistic grounds, but the wording of relevant proverbs dating from at least the early seventeenth century points to sheep being the original subject (*English Proverbs*, 723).

# M**EA**T

MAP 12
# M<u>EA</u>T

The main distinction here is between the long **ee** sound which is used in Received Pronunciation and the **ay** found in the north-west, west, and south Midlands, the South-west, and part of the South.

**ee** in this word and many others now spelt with -*ea*- (such as CLEAN, BLEAT, LEAF, SPEAK) is a development dating from the later seventeenth century. Earlier, until the late Middle English period, the sound had been a form of 'long open *e*', transcribed in IPA [ɛ:]. (In order to produce this sound, imagine the word MET, with the *e* drawn out: in words such as MEAT the **e** had precisely its modern sound, though lengthened). Pronunciations similar to **ay** occurred from the late fifteenth century onwards. At first they were long, drawn-out 'close *e*' ([e:]) of the kind which occurred in SHEEP (that is, pronounced with the tongue higher in the mouth). The sound ultimately became diphthongized into various varieties of **ay** in many places, although in those parts of the West Midlands and central Southern England where **ay** is marked on the map the sound in fact has remained the 'long close *e*'. The historical development of the standard English sound was thus

$$1400 \text{ 'long open } e\text{'} \rightarrow 1550 \text{ 'long close } e\text{' and } \mathbf{ay} \rightarrow 1700 \text{ } \mathbf{ee}$$

The other pronunciation shown here, **i-uh**, is noted by Wright (*Dialect Grammar*, para. 59) as being a widespread dialectal development for MEAT and many related words.

The word MEAT is of interest in that it originally meant food in general, usually implying solid food as distinct from drink as in such surviving idioms as 'It's meat and drink to them'. It is in this sense too that MEAT survives in SWEETMEAT. Its first recorded use with the restricted meaning of the flesh of animals is in the fourteenth century (*Oxford English Dictionary*).

FLESH, the original English word for animals as food, continued in use in standard English alongside the increasingly popular MEAT for some 500 years, until at least the early nineteenth century: witness *Good King Wenceslas*, "Bring me flesh and bring me wine". In parts of Scotland and Ireland some people still call a butcher a FLESHER.

# R<u>OO</u>M

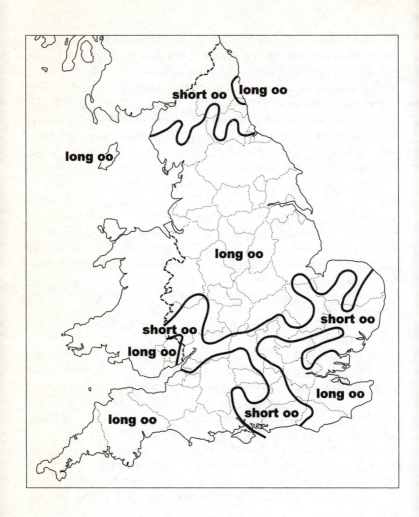

MAP 13

# R<u>OO</u>M

Historically the vowel-sound in ROOM, which dates from Old English times, has most regularly been **long oo**, so that the pronunciation which is seen to be used over most of the country is essentially that which has been heard for the word for between a 1,000 and 1,500 years. The use of **short oo** in ROOM is not well-documented historically, but it appears that it is a comparatively modern phenomenon dating perhaps from as late as the seventeenth or even the eighteenth century. At this period such words as BOOK, HOOD, and SOOT, which had in the later Middle and early Modern English periods been pronounced with **long oo**, came to be pronounced with **short oo**, and although ROOM was not properly part of this change it seems to have become connected with it for some speakers. Why the short sound in ROOM should have acquired the geographical distribution for the non-standard dialects which the map shows is quite unclear.

Although there is no firm evidence to support the claim, it is likely that the **short oo** innovation in ROOM acquired some considerable popularity for a while in Received Pronunciation. Today it ranks as a quite acceptable minor variant in that accent, but not long ago its status was even higher. Daniel Jones (*Outline of English Phonetics*, para. 318) writes that "In *broom* (for sweeping), *groom*, *room*, and *soot* both **u:** [**long oo**] and **u** [**short oo**] are heard, the **u**-forms **brum**, **grum**, **rum**, **sut** being perhaps more usual in Received English".

Today one would not expect an RP speaker to use **long oo** in SOOT. Conversely, although **short oo** is shown as an RP variant in pronouncing dictionaries of British English for use in several words with -*oo*- spellings, it is now somewhat unusual for such a speaker to be heard using it in BROOM, ROOM, and (especially) GROOM. In a survey of a somewhat less-than-representative sample of British English speakers, Wells (*Pronunciation Dictionary*) discovered an 82 per cent preference for **long oo** in ROOM and a 92 per cent preference for its use in BROOM.

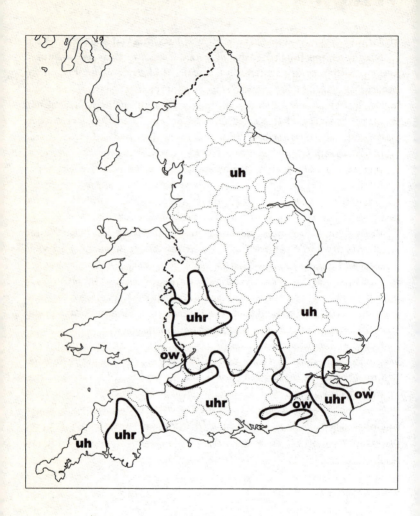

MAP 14
# YELL<u>OW</u>

The words MEADOW, SHADOW, SPARROW, WIDOW, and YELLOW all had final -we spellings in Middle English, spellings which represent a **-wuh** pronunciation, but as the Middle English period progressed the **uh** part of the pronunciation fell away, and the remaining -w was given an **oo** sound. This **oo** sound remained well into Modern English times, but gradually an -ow spelling came to replace the simple -w, and this new spelling came to influence the way the words bearing it were pronounced. This fact, a good example of the phenomenon known as *spelling pronunciation*, is evidence that literacy has resulted in pronunciations coming increasingly to be influenced by the way in which words are written.

Another group of words now spelt -ow had a different early history from those like SHADOW and YELLOW described above, but in most cases their more recent history has been the same. This group, which included BORROW, FOLLOW, HALLOW, and SORROW, had Middle English spellings with -l- or -r- followed by w, the w taking the place of an obsolete letter ȝ. This letter represented a consonant produced at the back of the mouth, similar to the final sound in the present-day Scots pronunciation of LOCH. In these cases a form of **ow** pronunciation developed directly without an intervening **oo** stage. It may only be coincidence that it is from this second set of words that examples of modern **ow**-only words (that is, words which do not have **-uh** or **-uhr** varieties) seem to come: alternatively it may be that their longer history of having **ow** pronunciations has had some influence.

In formal speech today the pronunciation of the final syllable reflects the standard spelling. In regional dialects and often in informal speech, however, this unstressed final syllable may be pronounced **uh**. According to Joseph and Elizabeth Wright (*New English Grammar*, para. 171), earlier **oo** and **ow** endings could normally be expected to have become **uh** in standard pronunciation, so that the sound used over much of the country in non-standard speech may be the result of a normal English development. **uhr** pronunciations have no historical or spelling significance, but are developments special to some areas where rhoticity is the norm (see ARM, Map 15).

MAP 15

# A<u>R</u>M

*Rhoticity* or *r-colouring*—the pronouncing of *r* either before a consonant or finally in such words as ARM, HORSE, TURN, FLOWER—was for a long time a regular feature of English pronunciation, which is why the letter *r* exists in those words when they are spelt today. However, the feature began to weaken in parts of southern England during the fifteenth century, as is shown by spellings of that time such as *Dosset* for DORSET. R-colouring finally ceased to be a feature of standard pronunciation in the eighteenth century.

Although many words kept the letter *r* when it ceased to be pronounced, others lost it. The names for the fish BASS and DACE originally contained *r*: BASS was originally Old English *bærs*; DACE was, in Middle English, *darse*, a word derived from *Old French*, the dialects spoken in the modern geographical area of France approximately from the mid-ninth to the fifteenth century (Joseph and Elizabeth Wright, *New English Grammar*, para. 189).

As can be seen from the map, absence of **r** in the non-standard dialects is particularly a feature of the eastern part of the country, and pronunciations without **r** are spreading rapidly, undoubtedly under the influence of Received Pronunciation, which is itself a *non-***rhotic** accent. Trudgill (*Dialects of England*, 51) indicates that only the North-west and South-west areas exhibit rhoticity in the most modern dialects, and his accompanying map indicates those areas to be considerably smaller than those shown here.

Traditionally three quite distinct types of *r* occur as r-colouring, each characteristic of different areas:

(i) A *retroflex* variety, produced with the tongue pulled back in the mouth and with its tip curled up, resulting in a particular deep, resonant **r**-sound. This is characteristic of the South-west and south-west Midlands.

(ii) A *fricative* variety, the usual **r**-sound in RP RED, made with the tongue flat and its top curled back. This is found in Lancashire and Yorkshire and in Kent.

(iii) A 'throaty' or *uvular* variety, sometimes called the 'Northumberland burr', found in the far North-east.

# CUSH<u>IO</u>N

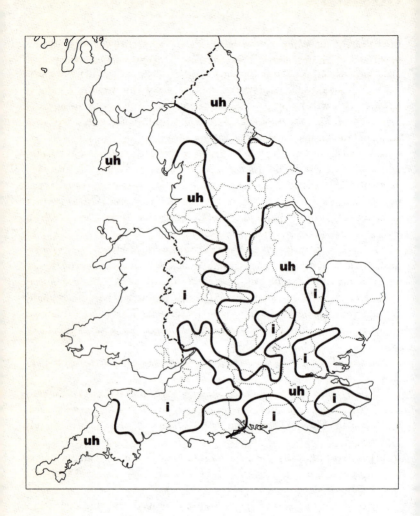

MAP 16
# CUSH<u>ION</u>

In English pronunciation the vowels *a*, *o*, and *u* in ***unaccented syllables***, that is in syllables which are not strongly stressed, are frequently ***reduced*** or ***weakened***. This means that instead of keeping the sounds which they have when emphasized (**a**, **o**, and **oo** respectively), they acquire the 'neutral', relaxed sound which in phonetic transcription is indicated by the symbol *schwa* [ə]. In this way DIALECT comes to be pronounced <u>da-i</u>-**uh**-**lekt** rather than <u>da-i</u>-a-lekt, and PHONETIC is usually pronounced **fuh**-<u>net</u>-**ik**, not **fo**-<u>net</u>-ik (where underlining indicates the strongly-stressed syllable and, in the absence of a schwa symbol in the alphabet, **uh** indicates [ə]).

It is this phenomenon which we can see at work in the pronunciation of CUSHION. The word entered English in the Middle Ages from Old French, where it had such forms as *cossin* and *cussin*, to become Middle English *cusshin*. The spelling implies that in the earliest English form of the word the **i** sound was retained in the second syllable, but reduction has resulted in the production of an **uh** form which, as the map shows, is popular over approximately half of England. This is the form which is most likely to be used by speakers of Received Pronunciation too. The strong survival of the old **i** pronunciation is probably due at least in part to the phonetic similarity of CUSHION to such **i**-words as PIGEON and WIDGEON, all three having ***palatal*** sounds, **sh** or **j**, in the middle (Ekwall, *English Sounds and Morphology*, para. 108).

Other words which in Middle English originally had **-in** endings have now generally acquired one fixed pronunciation. Some, which often have a modern spelling *-ine*, have kept **i**: DISCIPLINE, FAMINE, FEMININE, RUIN. Others with the *-ine* spelling, often those which Joseph and Elizabeth Wright (*New English Grammar*, para. 159) call 'learned words', have **a-i** or **ee** pronunciations: COLUMBINE, FELINE, PRISTINE. Still others, generally spelt with *-in*, have the reduced form **uh**: BASIN, COUSIN. Some *-in* words such as COFFIN and LATIN, which were once pronounced with **uh**, have acquired a modern **i** pronunciation under the influence of their spelling.

# TONGUE

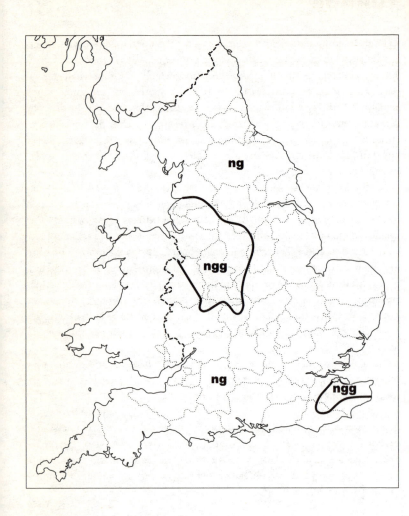

MAP 17

# TONGUE

Most English speakers make a distinction between the *ng* sound that occurs inside a word, or ***medially***, and that which occurs at the end of the word, or ***finally***. Medially, in a word such as FINGER, and in adjectives such as STRONGER, STRONGEST, the usual pronunciation is with the 'hard' *g* sounded, giving **ngg**. Finally, in words such as SING and TONGUE, there is not usually a 'hard' *g*, so that the sound is **ng**, with the **g** 'swallowed' instead of being given its full force. (When such a word as SING is added to by a ***suffix***, an **ng** pronunciation is normally kept, giving **singuh** rather than **singguh**.)

However, the map shows that speakers in at least two areas of England are unusual in that they use 'hard' *g* in all cases where *ng* occurs in the spelling, irrespective of whether this is inside or at the end of a word. In doing this they are preserving pronunciations which were for a very long time the norm in English. During the Old English period *ng* spellings invariably represented **ngg** pronunciations. This remained so for most of the Middle English period too. In the late Middle English period however, that is during the fifteenth century, it appears that word-final **ng** pronunciations came increasingly to be used (Joseph and Elizabeth Wright, *New English Grammar*, para. 270). It is these which are found in Received Pronunciation and in most other accents today. Sometimes, especially in areas beyond those which can be considered as the heartland of the **ngg** phenomenon, speakers use the feature variably: some Sheffield speakers, for example, will say **singguh** for a person who sings, but **singuh**, without the 'hard' *g*, for the trade name of a sewing machine or car.

Although the **ngg** pronunciation is a very ancient one it is remarkably persistent, showing little sign of disappearing from its location in the West Midlands and the southern North-west. It is a characteristic which can readily be used to identify very many speakers of modern West Central dialects. Trudgill (*Dialects of England*, 56) makes the point that natives of BIRMINGHAM pronounce the name of their city **Birming-g'm**.

# <u>W</u>OOL

MAP 18

# WOOL

The English sounds **w** and **y** are technically classed not as vowels or consonants but as *semivowels*, sounds which occur at the beginning or end of syllables and in which an initial vowel sound (**oo** and **i** respectively) immediately gives way to another vowel sound of as much or greater prominence. Although we usually think of these sounds as being consonants, their vowel-like quality means that they frequently disappear in non-standard speech when they occur alongside a vowel. This is especially the case when they occur at the beginning of a word and precede their vowel equivalent (**oo**, **i**). As can be seen from the map, there is a regional aspect to this phenomenon, although it is unclear why this is so.

In WOOL, the vowel sound following **w** is **short oo**, and the initial **w** is 'swallowed up' by the **oo** sound in the accents characteristic of a considerable part of England. The occurrence of this dropping of **w** in areas of England bordering Scotland and Wales would suggest that it takes place in these countries too, and this is indeed the case. In fact, absence of **w** in such words as WOOL and WOMAN would probably be regarded by many as particularly characteristic of the English speech of South Wales rather more than of South-west England.

It does not seem that this loss of semivowels under the influence of following vowels of similar quality is a particularly predictable feature of non-standard speech: its geographical occurrence varies from word to word, and between the two semivowels themselves. Comparison of the map for WOOL with another for WOMAN shows that the latter lacks a *no* **w** area in Northern England but that the South-western area is less fragmented than that for WOOL and extends further north in the West Midlands. Analogous loss of initial **j** in words such as YEAR is a feature of non-standard speech particularly in the North and the West Midlands rather than of that in the South-west, where its occurrence is limited to the extreme south of Cornwall.

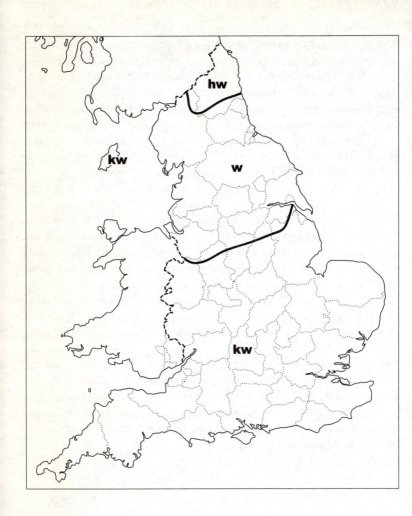

MAP 19

# the <u>QU</u>ICK of the fingernail

The original meaning of QUICK in Old English, where its form was *cwic* or *cwicu*, was 'living', 'alive', and it is in this sense that it has been preserved in the designation of the skin surrounding the base of the fingernail as the QUICK, skin which, if broken, is extremely sensitive. This use is the only survival of something approaching the original meaning of QUICK in Modern English, but many people are still familiar with somewhat archaic Bible and Prayer Book references to 'The quick [i.e. living people] and the dead', in which the precise original meaning is preserved.

Although the standard form of QUICK with **kw-** is found throughout England, the **w-** form WICK maintains a strong presence in Northern England generally. There is probably a twofold reason for this. First, as can be seen by comparing this map with that for ACTIVE (Map 45), there is widespread use of WICK to describe an active person, notably in Durham, Teesside, and parts of Yorkshire and Lancashire, this use reinforcing the WICK form in its association with the fingernail. Secondly, at a historical level, non-standard WICK, which is descended from Old Norse as are many northern and eastern English words, can refer to the corner of the mouth or eye, and there is considerable similarity between the skin surrounding the mouth and eye and that found at the base of the fingernail. Curiously, it can be noted in this connection that a **kw-** form, QUICK OF THE LIPS, is still used in Surrey to refer to the corners of the mouth.

**hw-** is a characteristic Scots pronunciation of words whose spelling begins with *wh-*, and it is to be expected that such words as WHEEL, WHIP will begin with **hw-** in that part of Northern England adjoining Scotland. Although QUICK does not of course begin with *wh-*, it appears that some speakers in that area analyse the northern WICK form as doing so and use the **hw-** pronunciation as a result. The **hw-** pronunciation is discussed in relation to WHELP in the commentary for the map of PUPPY (Map 65).

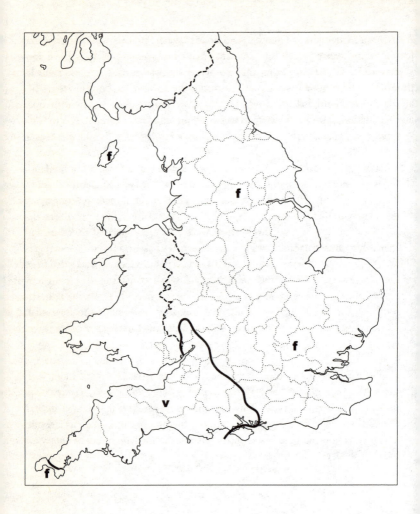

MAP 20

# FINGER

A **v** in place of an expected standard **f** at the beginning of words is a well-known feature of pronunciation in the South-western counties of England, affecting such words as FATHER and FARMER. It is the result of *voicing* the sounds, that is of pronouncing them with vibration of the vocal cords: in traditional dialects it affects a set of sounds called *fricatives*, which are consonants pronounced with audible friction, turning *voiceless* versions into *voiced* ones as follows:

| voiceless | | voiced |
|-----------|---|--------|
| **f** | → | **v** |
| **s** | → | **z** |
| **sh** | → | **zh** (the final sound in GARAGE) |
| **th** | → | **dh** (the 'hard' *th* sound in THIS) |

This feature of South-western pronunciation was once much more wide-spread in Southern England than it is today. The process must have become established at an early stage in the development of the language, because the words which are affected by it are usually those derived from Old English: most French words introduced after the Norman conquest do not exhibit voicing, even in the South-west (a notable exception being FARMER). In a few words such as VIXEN (Old English *fyxen*) the voiced non-standard dialect pronunciation has become the standard form: as Wright states (*Dialect Grammar*, para. 278), "there is no evidence that *vixen* ever has **f** in any dialect".

The use of **f** found at the very tip of Cornwall is a good example of the late learning of English in the area (see FIND, Map 9).

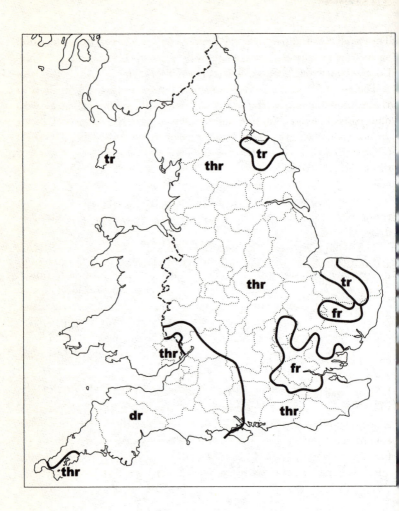

MAP 21

# THREE

The voiceless *th* heard in THREE in RP is also heard in non-standard accents over most of the country, including south-east Wales and the south-western tip of Cornwall where English was learned comparatively late.

The use of **d** in such *th-* words as THISTLE and **dr** in such *thr-* words such as THREE is a traditional feature of pronunciation in the South-west and indeed other parts of southern England, and seems to be related to the fricative voicing phenomenon which is discussed in the commentary for FINGER (Map 20). Wright (*Dialect Grammar*, para. 313) points out that the usual development of voiceless **thr-** in these areas is to **dr-**, rather than to the voiced **dhr-** (*th* of THAT, + *r*) which would be expected simply as a result of fricative voicing. Wells (*Accents of English*, 343) asserts that **dhr-** never occurs, and although this overstates the case it is reasonable to suggest, as Wright does, that when it does occur it is as a result of **dr-**-speakers trying to pronounce the **thr-** of 'literary English'.

The sound **tr** is recorded in THREE by Wright in the areas of eastern England and the Isle of Man which exhibit it on the map, and also in Lancashire, where the Survey of English Dialects did not collect it.

The use of **f** in place of RP **th**, irrespective of whether the sound is at the beginning (THREE), in the middle (ARTHUR), or at the end (BATH) of a word, is well known as a feature of London 'Cockney' speech but is seen to be located more widely in the Home Counties and Suffolk. As a feature of London speech it is discussed in detail by Wells (*Accents of English*, 328–9) under the heading ***TH Fronting***. In his discussion Wells makes the important point that although native Londoners all to some degree use **f** for **th** and, except at the beginning of words, **v** for **dh**, even the broadest Cockney speaker has available in her or his repertoire all the sounds involved, and does not therefore risk confusing FREE and THREE, FOUGHT and THOUGHT, LAVA and LATHER. Wells also points out the value of TH fronting to advertising copywriters: "Advertisements for beer award the brand in question 'thirst prize', or declare that 'for the southerner, it's the guv'nor'."

# CABBA**GE**

MAP 22

# CABBA<u>GE</u>

The variation in the pronunciation of the final consonant in CABBAGE is a case where alongside the modern sound there exist both the sound from which it has derived and a further non-standard development.

CABBAGE is first recorded in Middle English as *cabache* (incidentally descended from the Old French word for 'head'). The final sound in the word, represented by the spelling *-che*, was **ch**, and it is this sound which can be seen to have survived in a considerable area of the West Midlands. Middle English **ch** has generally passed into Modern English unchanged irrespective of the position in which it is found in a word, so that, for example, CHEAP, DUCHESS, and PREACH have the same sound in earlier and later forms of the language.

However, when the Middle English **ch** occurred after a vowel sound which was unaccented, not receiving emphasis in the pronunciation, in Modern English it has regularly become **j**. Since the accent or emphasis falls at the beginning of CABBAGE, i.e. <u>CAB</u>BAGE, the standard final sound is now **j** rather than **ch**. It is this rule that has turned Anglo-Norman *saussiche* into standard Modern English SAUSAGE, and which also, in spite of their modern spellings, leads many of us to find such words as SPINACH and the place-names GREENWICH, NORWICH, and HARWICH with **j**.

It is not clear precisely why the **sh** pronunciation arose in Northern England. It is essentially a simplification of **ch**, since the **ch** sound is made up of the two separate sounds **t** + **sh**, and the northern form has lost the first of these. Whatever the reason for its existence, it clearly has strong roots. Wright (*Dialect Grammar*, para. 366) records the **sh** pronunciation in CABBAGE in Cumberland and Yorkshire, and the **ch** pronunciation in Lancashire, Cheshire, and Derbyshire.

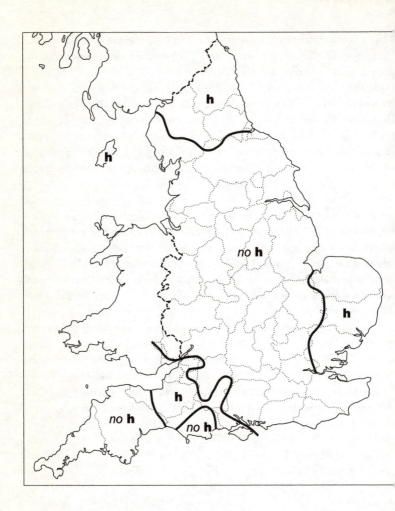

MAP 23

# <u>H</u>OUSE

The subject of this map is ***h-deletion***, the dropping of the **h** sound at the beginning of a word spelt with the letter *h*. This phenomenon is well known to occur in non-standard varieties of English speech and is one of the most fundamental ways in which such varieties can differ from RP. It is clear from this map, however, that there are areas of northern, eastern, and south-western England where **h-** has traditionally been retained by most, if not all, speakers.

Whereas the **h**/**h**-less distinction was originally important geographically, it seems likely that factors other than region are today more important in determining whether a speaker uses initial **h** or deletes it. This is certainly the case in Norwich, extensively studied by Trudgill, which, although it is firmly located in a historically **h**-using area, "has in fact been h-less for the last 70 years at least" (*On Dialect*, 77). Trudgill's descriptions of Norwich h-deletion are readily available in *On Dialect* (76–8) and *Dialects in Contact* (10–11). There, h-less speech is shown to be working-class speech. Furthermore, the readiness of a speaker to delete **h** or to use it is strongly influenced by the formality of the context in which they are speaking and therefore by the degree to which they are monitoring their pronunciation: a high degree of awareness of speech, occurring in formal situations, leads to avoidance of forms which are likely to be stigmatized but which may be used in more relaxed, informal contexts. Language features of this kind, which are sensitive to considerations of ***style*** as well as to such social distinctions as class, sex, or age are, following William Labov, known technically as ***markers***, while those which may show variation according to social distinctions but which do not vary according to styles of usage are ***indicators***. Markers, then, are the result of linguistic sensitivity. In the case of h-deletion, or of the dropping of **g** from words spelt with final -*ng*, this sensitivity is clearly triggered by spelling: the existence of initial *h* in a word such as HOUSE, and of final *g* in RUNNING, results in speakers being aware that **h** and **g** are significant in their respective pronunciations and in their making the sounds when they are thinking carefully about their speech.

In many regional dialects loss of initial **h** is complemented by its addition in words beginning with a vowel, especially when such words are strongly stressed. An example of this deletion and addition is found in Osbert Sitwell's poem *Mrs Hague*: "Wednesday h'Alfred 'as 'is dinner h'early".

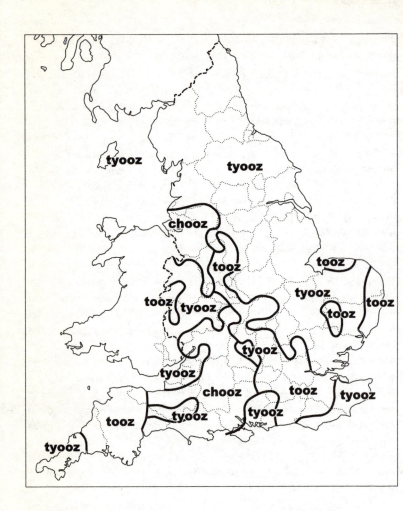

MAP 24

# <u>TUES</u>DAY

The standard or received pronunciation of this word begins with **tyooz**, and it is therefore not surprising that this is the sound characteristic of non-standard accents over approximately half of England. However, **tyooz** on the map masks the fact that in all those areas where it appears many speakers in fact have a **tiooz** pronunciation, and it is this **tiooz** which is the older sound in the word. TUESDAY is a day named after the Viking god Tiw, and the early pronunciation of the day, written *Tiwesday*, was **tiwzday**. In the sixteenth century **tiwz** became **tyooz** in standard speech, but both this and a modified form of **tiwz**, namely **tiooz**, have remained side by side as non-standard forms.

Once established as having a **tyooz** pronunciation, it was normal for TUESDAY to develop an initial **chooz** instead: **ty** becoming **ch** is a feature of the development of English pronunciation which has taken place since Shakespearian times and which is heard in such words as CREATURE, FORTUNE, NATURE, and VIRTUE. Those areas where **chooz** is found today are therefore those which subscribe to a quite ordinary and accepted sound-change. As Joseph and Elizabeth Wright point out in the *New English Grammar* (para. 185), adherence to **ty** is due to the influence of the spelling: speakers appreciate that the word is not spelt with *ch* and are therefore reluctant to pronounce it with a **ch** sound, and the **ty** (or **ti**) pronunciation is perpetuated in a community.

Spelling pronunciation no doubt accounts in part for the simple **tooz** pronunciations, and it is not hard to appreciate also that the **i** sound in a **tiooz** pronunciation could easily be overwhelmed, ceasing to be heard. Whatever the primary reason, it is a well-known feature of several dialects, and probably the best-known feature of dialects in East Anglia, that words with RP **yoo** have simply **oo**. Examples of this phenomenon include DUBIOUS, MUSIC, STUPID, and, from a well-known Norfolk turkey advertisement, BEAUTIFUL (**bootiful**).

Besides TUESDAY, words for three other weekdays derive from the Old English names of the Norse gods: WEDNESDAY from Woden (ON Odin), THURSDAY from Thunor (ON Thor), and FRIDAY from Woden's wife Frig (ON Frigg).

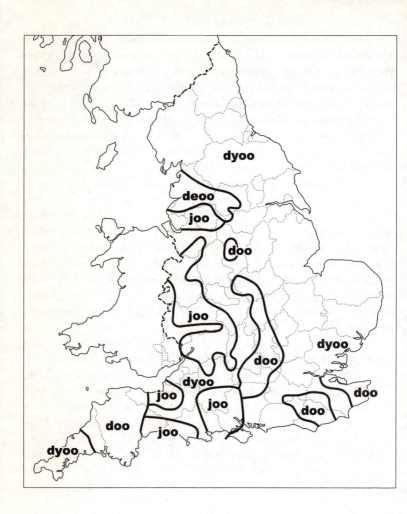

MAP 25

# DEW

The vowel sounds of DEW and TUESDAY (Map 24) were dissimilar throughout the Middle English period, but by the eighteenth century at the latest their sounds had converged. Because of their Modern English similarity and the similar effects which their vowels have had on the consonants preceding them, it is useful to compare the maps for the two words.

In both words an early **ioo**-type pronunciation tended over time to become **yoo**, although the development in DEW occurred as much as two centuries later than that for TUESDAY. The existence of both **dyoo** and **dioo** in twentieth-century non-standard dialects is masked in this map, as it is in the case of the **tyoo/tioo** distinction in TUESDAY, the difference between the two sounds being small and there being considerable intermingling of the two throughout the country. However, the small **deoo** area in Lancashire and Yorkshire represents a variation of the **dyoo** or **dioo** pronunciation which is sufficiently different to be worthy of particular note.

Just as a normal development of **ty** is to **ch**, so **dy** may be expected to become **j**: this is precisely what has happened in RP for the word SOLDIER. That this expected sound-change has not taken hold universally is due in large measure to the influence of spellings, which have remained fixed at forms such as *di* and *de* rather than making use of *j*. Although the **j** development has never become completely accepted, in the eighteenth century it was especially well supported, Joseph and Elizabeth Wright pointing out (*New English Grammar*, para. 185) that at that time such words as INDIA and ODIOUS were normally pronounced with **j** where today we might expect **dy** or **di**. Spelling also influences the simple **doo** pronunciations, interestingly not as widespread as is **too** in TUESDAY.

In his *Dialect Grammar* (para. 296) Wright says that the change from **dyoo** to **joo** has occurred in the same dialects in which **tyoo** has become **choo**. A comparison of the maps for DEW and TUESDAY shows that this is not entirely the case today, however. Although there are considerable correspondences, with **choo** and **joo** replacing **tyoo** and **dyoo** over much of the West Midlands and the Southwest, the matching is far from complete.

# GIVE IT ME

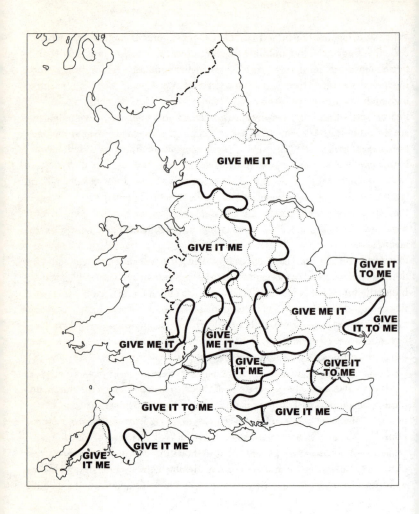

MAP 26
# GIVE IT ME

When studying variation between different expressions for GIVE IT ME we are concerned with *syntax*, the grouping together of words in order to express particular meanings. This can be contrasted with *morphology*, the structure of individual words and the way in which words change to express different meanings such as different verb tenses or a change from singular to plural. Morphological variation typically involves special endings or change within a word, as we see for example in the distinction between CAUGHT and CATCHED (Map 30) or between FLEAS, FLEN, and FLENS (Map 61). Syntax and morphology are the two branches of that part of language study which is usually known as *grammar*.

Although the Survey of English Dialects used the expression GIVE IT ME as the 'guiding expression' to indicate to fieldworkers the kind of response for which they were seeking, this word order is in fact not especially standard. Standard word order in such circumstances, where there are two objects or receivers of the action of the verb, is for the verb to be followed by the *indirect object*, this being followed in turn by the *direct object*. Identifying the two kinds of object can be done by removing each object in turn and asking what makes better sense. Is the basic structure of the command 'Give it' or 'Give me'? The answer is 'Give it', so that IT is the direct object, ME being the indirect object. (In the same way 'He built me a house' has HOUSE as the direct object, the basic structure being 'He built a house', not 'He built me'!) It follows from the basic rule that GIVE (verb) ME (indirect object) IT (direct object) would be somewhat more standard than GIVE IT ME.

GIVE IT TO ME, found most notably in the South-west, uses a standard device of putting the indirect object after the direct object and introducing it with a relationship-indicating *preposition*, in this case TO. (We can say 'He built me a house' or 'He built a house for me', FOR being the preposition here.)

Although the map shows the standard words ME and IT, these are often rendered respectively by US and EN, the latter, a descendant of the Old English IT-word *hine*, being found especially in South-west England.

## AMONG

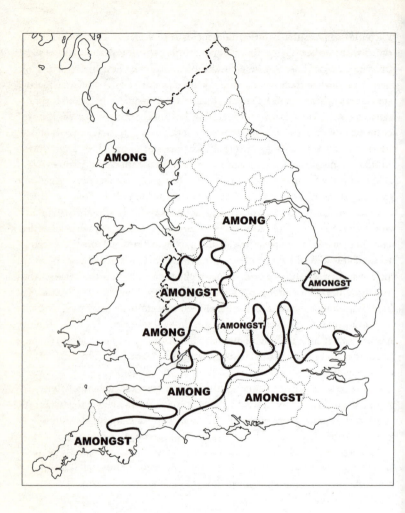

MAP 27

# AMONG

AMONG is the more usual word here, being used in all areas of England including those where AMONGST is shown on the map. In its original Old English form it was two words, *on* and *gemang* or *gemong* (in which the first *g* was pronounced like modern *y*), which in combination meant 'in a mixture'. The A- part of the word is simply an unstressed form of the Old English *on*, resulting from its being spoken without particular emphasis at the beginning of the larger word. The second part of the word had an independent existence for a long time. MONG, as a noun, was used to mean 'a mingling or mixture', for example of people or grain, in the Middle English period. It survived with this meaning in some non-standard dialects until still more recently, but it does not seem to be used today.

AMONGST is, as might be expected, a development of AMONG. During the Middle English period in particular pairs of words developed which differed only in the presence or absence of final *s*, this often signalling some slight difference in meaning. Sometimes the word with *s* was a new creation based on an earlier *s*-less form, as with BESIDES from BESIDE. Sometimes both words in the pair were new creations based on old components, as with BACKWARD(S) and FORWARD(S), (Maps 28 and 29). Some words which acquired an *s* like this went further, developing a *t* after the added *s*, resulting in such creations as AGAINST, AMIDST, WHILST, and the word which we have here, AMONGST. The tendency towards any phonetic change which makes it easier for a speaker to pronounce a word is known technically as ***euphony***.

It is interesting to note that, although it has a more restricted geographical spread than AMONG, the newer word AMONGST is well established in southern areas of England. It is, however, unclear as to whether it is encroaching on AMONG: the opposite may indeed be the case.

# BACKWARDS

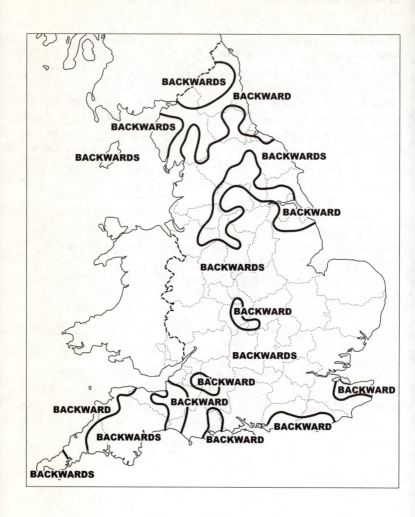

MAP 28
# BACKWARDS

The words BACKWARD and BACKWARDS were made up, in the Middle English period, from the stem ABACK and the suffix -WARD or -WARDS, meaning 'towards the place or direction specified'. Both suffix forms trace their existence back to Old English, when they were respectively -*weard* and -*weardes*.

Although the *Shorter Oxford English Dictionary* chooses BACKWARD as its headword and cites BACKWARDS as a variant form, it makes the point that when used ***adverbially***, to describe an action as here, it is the -WARDS form which is normally used today. This is seen to be the case in the non-standard dialects, BACKWARDS dominating over the whole country and in fact being found in every county, whilst BACKWARD occurs in scattered, albeit sometimes quite large, enclaves.

A regular sound change which occurred in the early Modern English period was for **w** to cease to be pronounced when it was at the beginning of the second part of a compound word. In this way HOUSEWIFE became HUSSIF, BOATSWAIN became BOSUN, and BACKWARD became BACKARD. Later, the tendency was to restore the **w** pronunciation wherever the letter *w* existed in spelling, but this was not done consistently. In the case of BOATSWAIN/BOSUN the **w**-less pronunciation prevails even when the former spelling is used, as it does in the pronunciation of place-names such as WARWICK and GREENWICH. Today BACKWARD and BACKWARDS show a preponderance of forms without **w** in the non-standard dialects, although this feature is by no means consistent and **w** is required in RP.

Other dialect words meaning BACKWARDS that have been recorded in the Survey of English Dialects include AFT and BACKSYFORE (Cornwall), ARSE-AFORE (Lancashire), ARSE-FIRST (Northumberland and Yorkshire), BACKING-ARSE (Yorkshire), and HEELWAY (Westmorland).

It is useful to compare this map with that for FORWARDS (Map 29).

# FORWARDS

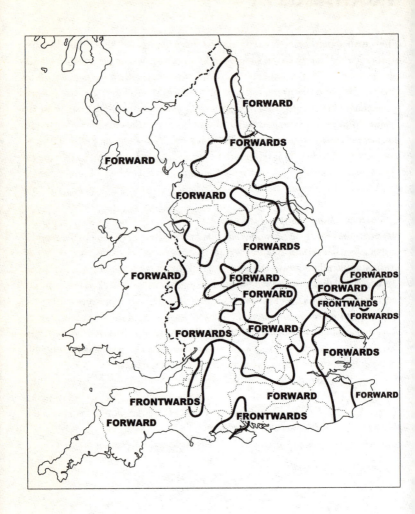

MAP 29

# FORWARDS

This map should be compared with that for BACKWARDS (Map 28). In this case distribution of the two forms FORWARD and FORWARDS is much more evenly balanced than that for BACKWARD and BACKWARDS. Each word occupies approximately the same amount of territory as the other, although FORWARDS is found somewhat more frequently in places mapped as containing FORWARD than vice versa. Additional to the closely contrastive forms FORWARD and FORWARDS, the form FRONTWARDS occupies sufficient ground for it to merit small distributional areas of its own. One remaining dialect synonym, FORTH, has been recorded in Cornwall.

Again, as with BACKWARDS, the *Shorter Oxford English Dictionary* gives the *s*-less form FORWARD as its principal headword and cites FORWARDS as a variant of it, whilst making the point in its discussion of the suffixes -WARD and -WARDS that the latter applies especially to adverbial use. (According to the dictionary, -WARD is especially used in the formation of adjectives; -WARDS, as well as being used in adverbial applications, tends to be found when contrasts are involved, and it should be noted that the responses under consideration here and at BACKWARDS were collected by means of a contrastive question which asked "There are two ways of walking. This way, I'm walking —— And this way, ——".)

Pronunciation of FORWARD, FORWARDS, and FRONTWARDS exhibits in somewhat stronger form the tendency to loss of **w** that is noted for BACKWARD and BACKWARDS. FORWARD thus becomes FORRARD, and FORWARDS becomes FORRARDS.

# CAUGHT

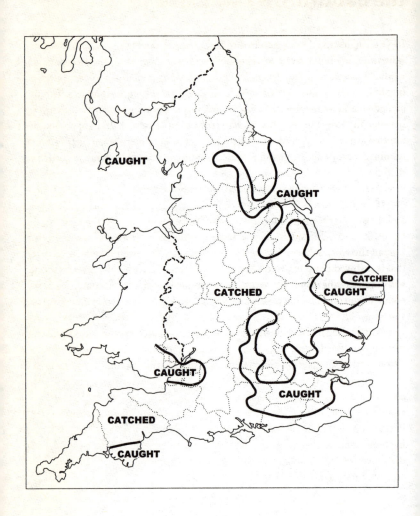

MAP 30

# the cat CAUGHT a mouse

In Old English, verbs fall into two distinct classes, one called either ***strong*** or ***irregular***, the other ***weak*** or ***regular***. Each class can be subdivided, and the whole situation is somewhat complicated: good explanations of the systems involved can be found in histories of English such as Baugh and Cable's *History of the English Language* and Strang's *History of English*. The essential difference between the two classes is that strong verbs indicated changes of tense through internal vowel change (Baugh and Cable, para. 46, cite SING–SANG–SUNG for infinitive, past tense, and past participles) while weak verbs added a sound, **t** or **d**, to the end of a basic ***stem*** (Baugh and Cable cite WALK–WALKED–WALKED). The weak verbs always formed the larger of the two classes.

The verb TO CATCH was introduced into Middle English from Anglo-Norman and, as is to be expected of a ***loanword***, entered the more common, weak/regular, class. Today's standard past-tense form CAUGHT is known to date from the time of the word's introduction into the language: although the vowel-change that is involved between CATCH and CAUGHT is an added complication its form, with the **t** ending, is clearly weak. The past-tense form CATCHED, which is of course formed in an entirely regular way, has probably also been in existence since the outset of the word's use in English: it is certainly known to have been very widely used in the early Modern English period. CAUGHT and CATCHED can therefore be seen to have equally valid English histories.

The history of the development of verb forms in English has essentially been one of ***regularization***, by which they increasingly come to signal tense differences in the same way by adding an ending to a basic, unchanging stem. So verbs coined to describe new actions, for example those ending in *-ize*, as REGULARIZE itself, or COMPUTERIZE, signal their past tenses by adding **d**, letter *-d,* whilst leaving their stems unchanged. Regularization and other issues concerning English dialect verb systems are discussed in depth by Trudgill and Chambers and their contributors in *Dialects of English*.

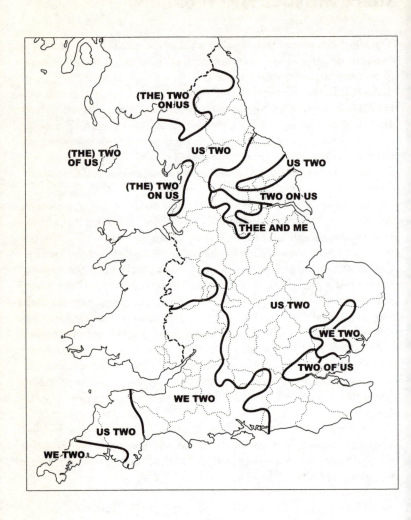

MAP 31

# there are just WE TWO

The main point of interest in this map is the contrast between WE TWO and US TWO: US TWO is often found in those parts of the North in which other mapped forms dominate, so that there is a clear two-way split in England.

According to *prescriptive* grammar which, unlike *descriptive* grammar, aims to explain what is 'correct' rather than simply to describe what people say, Standard English requires WE TWO here. This is because WE is a subject pronoun, and in the sentence 'There are just we two' WE TWO works as a *subject complement* which comes after the verb ('are') and says something about its subject. (In this curious kind of sentence the subject of the verb is merely a *prop subject*, 'there', and WE TWO explains what 'there' means.)

Although 'correct' Standard English requires WE TWO, however, it is not only speakers of non-standard dialects who can be expected to use the object pronoun US as the subject complement, producing the US TWO seen to be used by non-standard speakers over much of England. Contrasting 'it was he' (subject pronoun) and 'it was him' (object pronoun), Quirk and others in their *Grammar of Contemporary English* (para. 4.112) write: "Although the prescriptive grammar tradition stipulates the subjective case form, the objective case form is normally felt to be the natural one, particularly in informal style." On this same theme of the difference between formal and informal use of pronouns, Leech and others (*English Grammar for Today*, para. 11.4.4) write that "there is a considerable gulf between formal and informal English in the choice of pronoun forms", going on to describe the object pronoun as the *unmarked* or *neutral* pronoun which is quite likely to be used informally in place of a subject pronoun in many places in a sentence.

It is clear that, since there is a region in which the prescriptively correct WE TWO has traditionally been used, the distinction between WE TWO and US TWO has dialectal significance. That there is a debate in Standard English circles about such matters probably helps to account for the fact that, by using such forms as THE TWO OF (or ON) US, some speakers find ways of entirely avoiding use of a difficult and controversial construction.

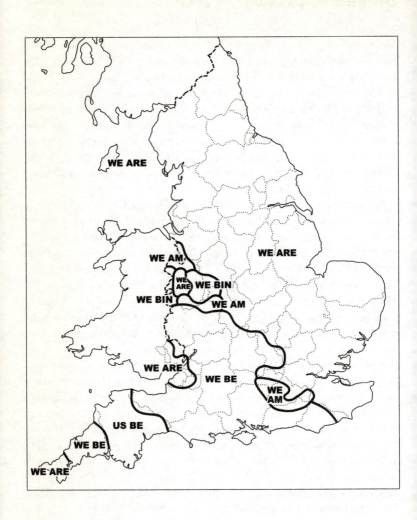

MAP 32

# oh yes WE ARE!

Shown here are ***contradictory positive*** expressions resulting from the question "If I say you people aren't English, you can contradict and say 'Oh yes …'". Because they were offered in contradiction to a statement, both the pronoun and the verb-form making up the expressions are in their stressed or ***emphatic*** forms.

The non-standard ***first person plural subject personal pronoun*** used over most of England in this situation is, as in Standard English, WE. In Devon, however, US, which in the standard dialect is strictly an object pronoun, is used instead: interestingly this feature is not remarked on by Joseph Wright in his dialect writings. Such examples of ***pronoun exchange***, whereby HE, SHE, IT, and THEY can act as objects and HIM, HER, US, and THEM can act as subjects of verbs, are a feature of dialects of the South-west. Discussing this phenomenon with many examples in *Dialects of England* (89–93), Trudgill states that in some dialects Standard English subject pronouns are used when the pronoun is emphasized: however, in Devon pronoun exchange seems traditionally to have held even under such circumstances.

As Trudgill (p. 98) remarks, the verb TO BE in English is highly irregular. Between them the standard and non-standard dialects show great variety in all tenses: the Standard English present tense alone has AM, ARE, and IS in the singular and ARE in the plural. In the situation shown, that for the ***first person plural, present tense***, WE ARE is of course the Standard English form, and this clearly dominates in Northern and Eastern England as well as in other small areas, notably where English was established comparatively recently. It is frequently the case that the singular/plural distinction is not made in verbs by non-standard speakers, so that WE AM can be expected to occur in places. Although now non-standard, the forms BE and BIN have sound English pedigrees, as their similarity to the ***infinitive*** form TO BE suggests. Both originate in Old English, were in use in Middle English, and in the forms *be* and *ben* were widely used into the seventeenth century (Ekwall, *English Sounds and Morphology*, para. 273). From that time onwards ARE, which is of both Old English and Old Norse parentage and which had until then existed alongside *be* and *ben* as an alternative form, became increasingly popular. Now the only survival of the earlier forms in Standard English is in the phrase 'the powers that be'.

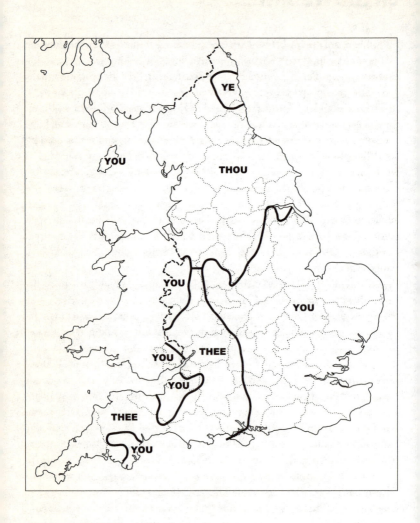

MAP 33
# YOU

The history of the ***second person personal pronoun*** YOU is a remarkable success story. Earlier forms of English had a system closely resembling that found in present-day French and many other modern languages, with separate singular (or familiar) and plural (or respectful) pronouns: using the French system as a model, linguists often call such an arrangement a ***tu-vous***, or simply a ***T-V***, system. Over the centuries, however, YOU has succeeded in supplanting the other pronouns of this system, THEE, THOU, and YE, and it is now challenging the ***impersonal pronoun*** ONE.

Many commentators have described the evolution of the present-day English second-person personal pronoun system. The following description paraphrases that to be found in Baugh and Cable, *History of the English Language* (para. 182), with extra information from Joseph and Elizabeth Wright's *New English Grammar* (para. 317).

In very early English there was a simple distinction between THOU for the singular and YE for the plural subject pronouns, while THEE and YOU were respectively used for the singular and plural object pronouns. In the thirteenth century the French T-V system came to be copied in English, singular *th*-forms being applied to familiars, children, and inferiors, while plural *y*-forms were used to show respect. By the sixteenth century the singular subject and object pronouns THOU and THEE had become interchangeable for many speakers. They also became increasingly unpopular, probably because of their connotations of disrespect, and gradually disappeared from standard speech, although they survived in the non-standard dialects and in the speech of egalitarian Quakers. YE and YOU were left as the standard pronouns applying to everyone, singular and plural, high and low, and they were of course used by some non-standard speakers also. These two surviving standard pronouns were frequently pronounced **yuh**, and like non-standard THOU and THEE they too came increasingly to be used interchangeably.

Since the sixteenth century, therefore, it has been quite possible to encounter THOU, THEE, YE, or YOU as subject pronouns as in this map, although given this complicated history it is remarkable that there remain such definite preferences for particular pronouns in different areas of England.

MAP 34
# SHE

SHE is used throughout England by standard and non-standard speakers alike as the ***third person singular feminine personal pronoun***, so it is not surprising to find it occupying most of the country. What is surprising, at least until the histories of the word and its synonyms are known, is the fact that speakers over a large area use an alternative word.

Before the Middle English rise to prominence of the ancestor of modern SHE, the most widespread word for 'she' was *hēo*. This form, with initial **h-** instead of the initial **sh-** which came to characterize the standard, has survived, becoming HOO or, through the h-deletion which occurs widely in non-standard speech, OO. (H)OO meaning 'she' is thus a word of considerably longer pedigree than is SHE itself.

That the personal pronoun SHE is not universally used in non-standard English is at least in part due to the fact that it did not come into widespread use in the language until early in the Middle English period. Its ancestry is somewhat problematic, but probably involves an alteration of the Old English feminine singular pronouns *hēo* or *hīe*, the former developing into the (H)OO/(SH)OO forms now confined to north-western areas, and the latter becoming the standard form SHE. Theories relevant to the development of today's third person feminine pronouns are discussed in Bennett and Smithers, *Early Middle English Verse and Prose* (xxxvi–xxxviii).

HER is of course found in modern Standard English, although there it is used only as the ***object*** or receiver of the action of a verb ('they found HER') while SHE is used as the ***subject***, the doer of the action ('SHE found them'). The use of HER as a subject pronoun, as here, has a likely historical base in Old English *hīe*, a close relative of *hēo*, which meant both 'she' and 'her'. Its survival meaning 'she' today may in part be aided by the tendency towards simplification in non-standard grammar: one pronoun (HER) for both subject and object is a reasonable simplification which can be effected without loss of understanding.

# HERS

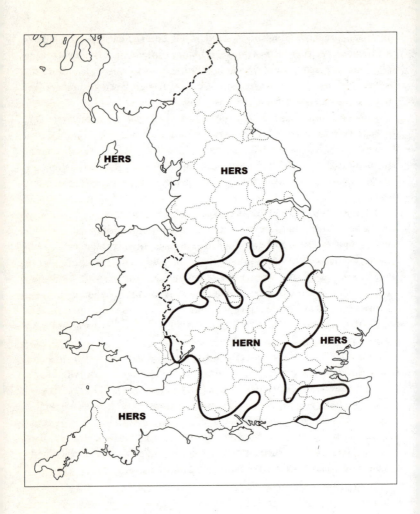

HERS

HERS

HERS

HERN

HERS

HERS

MAP 35
# HERS

HERS is a ***predicative*** possessive pronoun, which is placed after the subject of a sentence and makes a statement about to whom or to what that subject belongs. It is sometimes described as a ***disjunctive*** possessive pronoun: that is, it expresses the *separation* of something belonging to one person from that belonging to someone else ('that's hers *as opposed to* his'). Other predicative/disjunctive possessive pronouns are MINE, THINE, HIS, OURS, YOURS, and THEIRS.

Set alongside these pronouns are the ***attributive*** possessive pronouns, which precede the thing referred to and show possession to be an attribute of the thing possessed: not simply '*a* book' but '*my* book'. Because they are used in place of ***determiners*** such as A or THE, these pronouns are often themselves classified as determiners rather than as pronouns. The attributive possessive pronouns, sometimes also called ***conjunctive*** possessive pronouns because they *link* possession to the thing possessed, are MY, THY, HIS, HER, OUR, YOUR, THEIR.

In Old English and early Middle English predicative/disjunctive possessive pronouns were identical with the attributive/conjunctive possessive pronouns. In Middle English a tendency developed to use MINE and THINE before words beginning with a vowel, in order to make the transition from one word to another easier. Starting in the North in the late thirteenth century, and spreading throughout England by 1500, predicative and attributive possessive pronouns separated, with MINE and THINE becoming two of the predicatives; the others usually took the **-s** which regularly indicates possession, giving HERS from HER, OURS from OUR, and so on.

The form HERN, first recorded in the fourteenth century, is non-standard in taking the **-n** used in MINE and THINE instead of the more usual **-s**. Wright (*Dialect Grammar*, para. 413) notes this and other **-n** forms, writing that in "the midland, eastern, southern, and south-western counties the disjunctive pronouns are gen[erally] formed from the conjunctive by adding **n** or **ən**, thus *mine, thine, hisn, hern, ourn, yourn, theirn*". As Trudgill points out in *Dialects of England* (83), speakers who have traditionally used these pronouns have a system which, unlike that of Standard English with its mixture of **-s** and **-n** endings, is "entirely regularized".

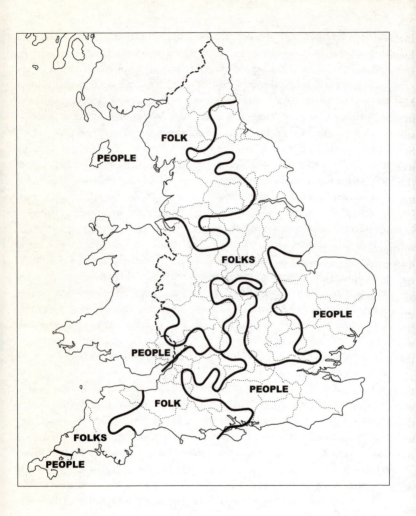

MAP 36
# PEOPLE

In this map we see an example of the surprising failure of a well-known Standard English word to make significant progress in the face of traditional non-standard speech forms.

PEOPLE is in origin an Anglo-Norman word, and was therefore first used in the Middle English period. As with many French-derived words it has supplanted its native English rival as the standard form, and yet somewhat untypically it has still to make significant progress in non-standard speech much beyond the South-east, though it is of course well known by all speakers of non-standard as well as of Standard English. It is interesting to compare PEOPLE with AUTUMN (Map 77), which, though restricted in range, seems to be making greater inroads into areas where English-derived words are strong.

FOLK, Old English *folc*, either in its original *s*-less plural form or in its somewhat later form with final -*s*, continues to occupy the majority of the country. The word always lacked final -*s* in Old English, as did other single-syllable words denoting collectivity, weight, measure, and time, for example DEER, SHEEP, SWINE, POUND, YEAR (Joseph and Elizabeth Wright, *Middle English Grammar*, para. 331). Standard English has of course preserved this rule for many such words, though others such as POUND and YEAR regularly take an -*s* today. However, the traditional dialects have preserved the rule even more consistently with those words which now take -*s* in the standard when they are preceded by a number, so that it is not unusual to hear 'five pound of potatoes' or 'three year ago'.

In the light of the non-standard retention of historical forms without -*s* it is particularly interesting to note that FOLKS, which is both unhistorical and at variance with the standard FOLK, is used as widely as it is. It appears that FOLKS was formed during the Middle English period at a time when such words as POUND and YEAR were being pluralized with -*s*, and that the form has been retained in many non-standard dialects after ceasing to be current in the standard.

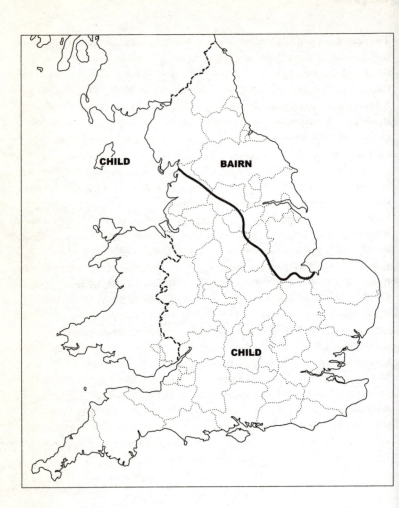

MAP 37
# CHILD

The neat division of England into a northern BAIRN area and a southern and Midland CHILD area is somewhat misleading. CHILD is found in widespread use in all but the most northerly areas of the country, whilst the mapped CHILD area contains within it a region centred upon Devon and Cornwall and extending into Somerset and Dorset where a variant, CHIEL, is recorded. BAIRN is apparently retreating northwards in the face of the dominant CHILD, and of course other colloquial words, KID and YOUNGSTER, are widely used too. Nevertheless, BAIRN is notably persistent in late twentieth-century northern English speech.

Both BAIRN and CHILD are Old English in origin, the former being Old English *bearn* and the latter *cild*. However, while BAIRN has always had only the restricted meaning of 'a young person, a son or daughter', CHILD, even in its earliest manifestations, has had a variety of meanings, this diversity suggesting that it has always been the dominant word. Although it is not certainly the case, it is likely that this dominance of CHILD over BAIRN has always been *spatial* or geographical as well as *semantic* or concerned with meaning. Besides its modern meanings CHILD has meant, amongst other things, 'a youth of gentle birth' (as in Byron's *Childe Harold*), 'a chorister', 'a man, a lad', and conversely 'a female infant'. In this last connection, and illustrating the use of both CHILD and BAIRN, note Shakespeare's *Winter's Tale*, "A very pretty barne. A boy or a child, I wonder?".

The standard plural of CHILD, CHILDREN, is a rare example of an English *double plural*. In Old English the plural of *cild* had been *cildru*, which in Middle English became *cildre*. This came to be commonly conceived as a member of a group of words which had singular forms ending in *e*, the plural of which was created by adding *n*. This *n*, added erroneously to pluralize a *cildre* which was already plural, created the word we have today. Middle English *cildre* survives as CHILDER in many parts of Lancashire today.

# GRANDAD

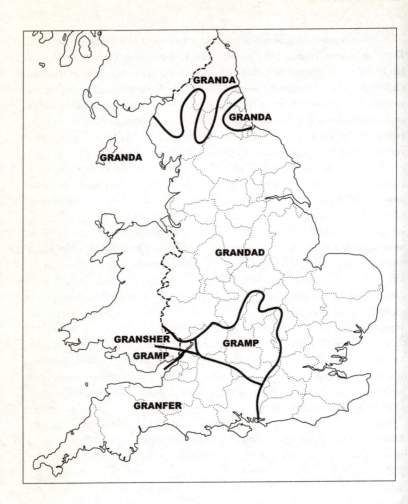

MAP 38

# GRANDAD

Those words mapped here which are referred to in the *Shorter Oxford English Dictionary* are given quite recent datings there, none being recorded before the late eighteenth century. This is not particularly odd, since regular use of familiar, children's words for a grandfather can be expected to have been uncommon in writing. Much more common will be the use of adults' formal words such as GRANDFATHER and GRANDSIRE, both of which date from the Middle English period, as does the use, following French practice, of GRAND- to indicate a family relationship at one remove in age from that of a parent.

The words which are specifically treated by the dictionary are GRANDAD, GRAMP, and GRANFER. GRANDAD, recorded from the late eighteenth century, is not surprisingly the most popular word, known to and used by speakers in all parts of England, since it is a simple combination of the GRAND- prefix and DAD, the common familiar word for father used since at least the sixteenth century. GRAMP and GRANFER both have dates of first recording in the late nineteenth century, although they are doubtless much more than a century old. GRAMP, with its variant forms GRAMPY and GRAMPS, is an altered version of the formal GRANDPAPA. Similarly GRANFER, which in this map is taken to include some examples of the closely-related words GRAMFER and GRAMFY, is a simple contraction of the formal GRANDFATHER.

Not dealt with in the *Shorter Oxford English Dictionary* are GRANDA and GRANSHER. The latter is undoubtedly a survival of the old word GRANDSIRE, while the former is a contraction of GRANDADA, a word recorded from the late seventeenth century: DA, 'father', is recorded from the mid-nineteenth century, marked in the dictionary as 'nursery and dialectal'.

Other familiar words for 'grandfather' are GAMP, GRANDPOP, GRANFY, PAP(PY), and POP. The well-known name GRANDPA appears traditionally to have been used in southern and eastern England but not to have commanded strong geographical loyalty anywhere. The most popular familiar words for 'grandmother' are GRAN, GRANMA, GRANMAM, GRANNY, and NANNY, to which list can be added such words as BABA, GANNY, GRAMMER, GRAMMY, GRANDMUM, and NANNA.

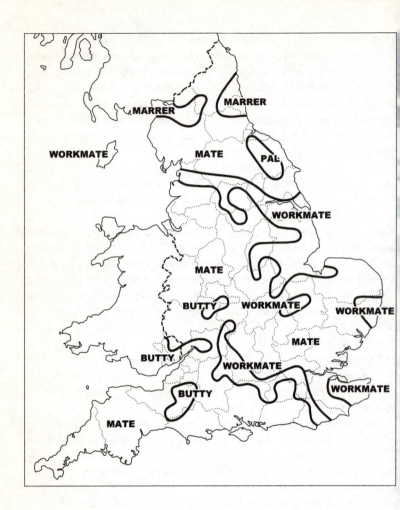

MAP 39

# WORKMATE

The Survey of English Dialects collected information on words used for three closely linked areas of social connection outside the family, those denoting a working association (WORKMATE), close leisure-time friendship (PAL), and looser familiarity (FRIEND). As is to be expected, words used in these *semantic fields* are to a large extent interrelated, and BUTTY, MATE, and PAL are used to indicate all three relationships. Preceding MATE with WORK- is of course a simple way of making clear reference to a working association, though it is remarkable that this should occur on a regional, albeit fragmented, basis.

MATE, in its original Middle English form, has as its base the prefix Y-, which denotes association, and is related to MEAT in its old sense of 'food': the original sense of the word was 'messmate, a person one eats with'. From this has come a variety of meanings, ranging from 'fellow worker'—a comparatively early use of the word—to 'friend', 'breeding partner', and 'assistant to a ship's officer'. Like MATE, MARRER, which is sometimes written MARROW or MARRA, is first recorded in use in Middle English, but this seems to derive from an Old Norse word *margr* 'many', which developed a figurative use 'friendly, communicative', its likely Norse origin being supported by its use in areas of known Viking settlement. Unlike MATE, which has expanded in meaning, MARRER has apparently contracted, now applying specially to people with whom one works.

Both PAL and BUTTY are of more recent English origin than are MATE and MARRER. PAL derives from *plal*, 'brother' in **Romany**, the language of gypsies. Indicative of the prejudice traditionally faced by gypsies, prejudice which has led to them being suspected of illegal or antisocial activities, is the fact that an early (seventeenth-century) meaning of PAL was 'accomplice'. BUTTY dates from the eighteenth century, and has long had associations with the workplace, especially the coal-mine, sometimes with reference to specific jobs. A localized dialect word in England and Wales, BUTTY lives on in North America in everyday colloquial speech as BUDDY.

It is interesting to speculate on which 'friendship' words are used by both men and women, and which are used to indicate male-only links.

# GYPSY

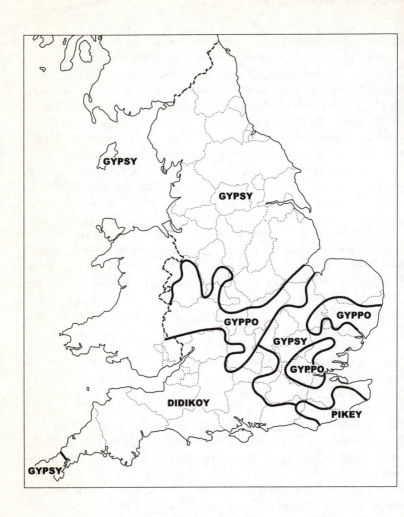

MAP 40

# GYPSY

GYPSY, the Standard English word which is found throughout England, is given its variant spelling GIPSY in the records of the Survey of English Dialects: correct English spelling is not always as fixed as is sometimes suggested. The word is a reduced form of EGYPTIAN, gypsies having once been thought to have come to Britain from Egypt. The reduction by which GYPSY derives from EGYPTIAN is partly *aphetic*, the initial unaccented vowel sound being lost.

GYPSY has given rise to a number of similar forms in the non-standard dialects. The variant shown on the map, GYPPO, would doubtless be regarded as a derogatory term if used in Standard English, but with the single exception of an informant in Essex there is no evidence that it is used insultingly by non-standard speakers. Other variants are GYP in Worcestershire and Lincolnshire, GYPPOT in Herefordshire, and GYPPY in Essex.

Like GYPSY, DIDIKOY has other accepted spellings such as DIDAKAI and DIDDI-COY, which is not surprising since the word seems to be derived from seldom-written Romany or gypsy language. Whilst not found as widely as GYPSY, DIDIKOY is used extensively throughout Southern England and has given rise to several variants: DICKOY in Shropshire, DIDDIK in Devon, DIDDIKITE in Somerset, Berkshire, and Surrey, DIDDY in Oxfordshire, Surrey, and Hampshire. Although it may superficially seem to be connected with DIDIKOY, DINLOE, recorded once in Hampshire, is more likely to be connected with the Travellers' word, sometimes spelt DINLOW or DINGLOW, meaning 'stupid', which has somehow been acquired by an informant and misapplied. ROMANY is the gypsies' own name for themselves as well as for their language but does not seem to be widely used to mean GYPSY by others, though it has been found in Yorkshire, Worcestershire, Lincolnshire, Norfolk, and Essex,

PIKEY, or PIKEE, is a word formed from TURNPIKE, historically a toll-road along which gypsies and others travelled. It is recorded by the *Shorter Oxford English Dictionary* as a variation on PIKER, used from the mid-nineteenth century onwards to refer to various itinerant people. Travelling people use the word insultingly amongst themselves to denote travellers of a lower caste. A more picturesque description is TURNPIKE-(ROAD-)SAILORS from Worcestershire. Inventive too is GANGING (i.e. 'going')-FOLK, recorded in Cumbria.

# ARMPIT

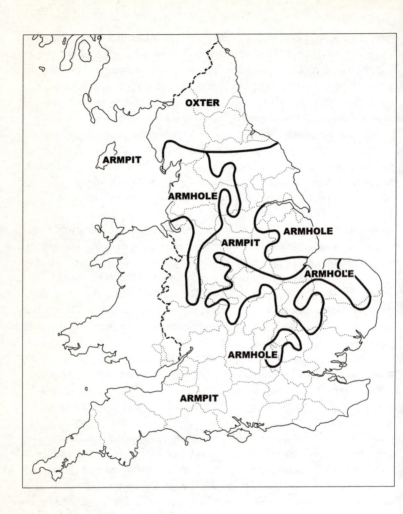

MAP 41

# ARMPIT

The scattered nature of the ARMHOLE areas on the map suggests that the word originally occupied all of Midland and much of Northern England, but that the standard word ARMPIT has eroded it from the south. At times ARMPIT is replaced by phrases such as PIT OF YOUR ARM. In the East Midlands UNDER-ARM is sometimes used, and also, especially in the Midlands, phrases such as UNDER or UNDERNEATH YOUR ARM are to be found.

It is quite easy to see how the second parts of the *compound* words ARMHOLE and ARMPIT, that is -HOLE and -PIT, have come to be applied to the hollow underneath the arm: like very many other words, standard and non-standard, they are built up by combining two or more smaller words, and are purely descriptive. However, the curious compound ARMFLOP has been collected in one place in Devon, and in this case the reason for the second element is unclear. This is so with many other words collected in dialect investigations. Sometimes a word may be offered by only one speaker, and the suspicion must remain that it is a *nonce-word* produced only for the dialect interview, or that it is used only by the speaker who was interviewed.

The Northern English word OXTER, which is also to be found in Scotland and Ireland, is descended from the Old English word *ōxta* or *ōhsta*. Although it never seems to have been used in England outside the most northerly area, it can be seen to have retained quite a strong presence there. It would be most interesting to investigate the present-day survival of such words as this, words which have been strongly supported by many traditional dialect speakers in a well-defined area but which have been little known in the country at large.

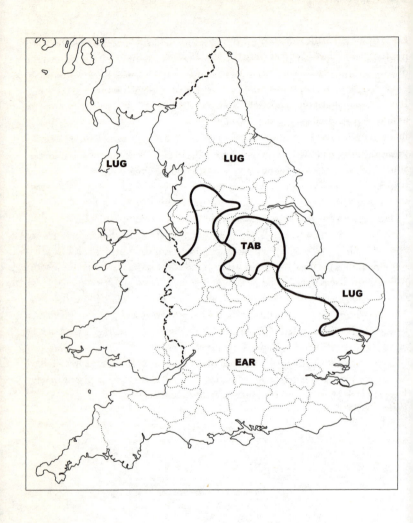

MAP 42

# the human EAR

EAR is the oldest of the words shown, coming from the Old English period. Since it is the standard word as well as being used in many non-standard dialects, it is of course widely used in the North and East where other words predominate.

LUG can be seen to be firmly established in the North and in the East Midlands. It is also a word that one can expect to hear elsewhere as a *colloquialism*, that is a word which is used in everyday casual conversation but which is not used in formal speech or writing. LUG probably comes from Scandinavia. If this is so it is just possible that it has been in use in the areas in which it is now well established since the Vikings settled there, though it is not recorded in use in English before the late fifteenth century. This first recorded use refers to one of the flaps of a hat covering the ears, but by the early sixteenth century at the latest the word had come to refer to the ear itself.

It is not surprising to find the human ear described in the dialects as a TAB, since although the *Shorter Oxford English Dictionary* does not define the word as meaning an ear it does give us the definition 'a small flap projecting from an object', adding that it is a projection 'by which the object may be taken hold of'! Of course LUG, and EAR itself, can also be used to describe a projection by which something is held. TAB seems to be related to TAG, which is a word used for an ear in Leicestershire.

Unmapped words for EAR include the descriptive FLAPPER from Essex, and the functional HARKER, HARKENER, and LISTENER from, respectively, Kent, Shropshire, and Staffordshire. WICKER does not allow of any explanation but has been found in both Gloucestershire and Kent. Parts of the human body are frequently given inventive, even 'jokey' names. For example, the head may be the CHUMP, NAPPER, or NODDLE, and the nose may be the CONK, CRONK, HUD, JIMMY, PECKER, SNECK, SNITCH, SNITCHER, SNOTTER, SNOUT, or TRUNK.

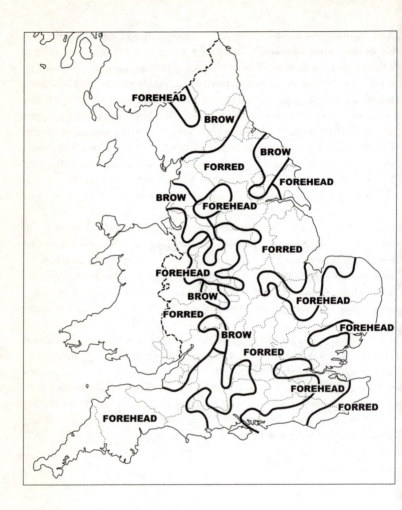

MAP 43

# FOREHEAD

Although the three forms shown on this map are presented as if they are three words, there are in fact two kinds of distinction to be made. First, there is a difference in *lexis* or vocabulary between FOREHEAD/FORRED and BROW. Secondly, there is a difference in *phonology* or pronunciation in the distinction between FOREHEAD and FORRED, which are of course forms of the same word.

Both BROW and FOREHEAD existed in the Old English period, although probably only FOREHEAD had precisely its present meaning at that time. BROW, as Old English *brū* (pronounced **broo**), seems to have been used in the plural to refer restrictively to eyelashes or eyebrows. It is not until the Middle English period that the word, in the singular, is recorded as denoting a person's entire forehead. In the change in pronunciation between Old and Modern English versions of BROW we have an excellent example of one of the notable and most accessible features of a set of English sound changes, which is often called the *Great Vowel Shift*. This took place in the fifteenth and sixteenth centuries, and is one of the factors leading to a marked difference between the English of Chaucer, who wrote in the fourteenth century, and that of Shakespeare writing in the late sixteenth and early seventeenth centuries. As part of this 'shift', the long **oo** sound, written *ū*, underwent breaking or fracture, the long single sound becoming the two sounds of the diphthong **a-oo**. It is in this way that such words as HOUSE and MOUSE acquired their modern standard pronunciations, having in Old English been pronounced respectively **hoos** and **moos**—pronunciations which today are still associated with north-eastern English and Scots.

In contrast to BROW, FOREHEAD has had its present meaning from Old English times. The spelling FOREHEAD sometimes represents a pronunciation **fawhed**, but it often disguises a **forrid** pronunciation, this latter being the form which is represented by FORRED on the map. It is not known when the **forrid** pronunciation arose, but it is now regarded as being slightly more standard than the alternative. The fragmentation of the BROW and FOREHEAD areas on the map suggests that both forms are in decline in the face of the popular FORRED.

# MOLARS

MAP 44
# MOLARS

It is striking that of the nine words mapped here five, namely BACKTEETH, DOUBLETEETH, GRINDERS, JAWTEETH, and MOLARS itself, are clearly descriptive either of position (BACKTEETH, JAWTEETH), formation (DOUBLETEETH), or function (GRINDERS, MOLARS). CHOCKTEETH too is probably named from the form of such teeth, since CHOCK is widely used in English to denote a block or lump of something.

Of the words which have descriptive explanations only one, the standard MOLARS, requires discussion. MOLARS is, in fact, a 'learned' late medieval equivalent of the more prosaic GRINDERS, being an English version of Latin *molaris*, which meant both a molar tooth and a grindstone and which derived originally from Latin *mola*, 'a mill'. It is interesting to see that, although MOLARS is the Standard English word, its use in traditional non-standard dialects is especially prevalent in only one area, although it is of course known and used by speakers throughout England. It is also worth noting that many instances which are recorded here as MOLARS in fact represent MAULERS, that is the pronunciation **mawlers**. This suggests that the large blunt teeth in question are regarded as being used to maul or mangle food, and if this is so the force which is at work here is ***folk etymology***, which is discussed in the commentary for GOOSEBERRY (Map 67).

The remaining words, AXLETEETH, EYETEETH, and JACKTEETH, are mysterious. AXLETEETH is in precisely the northern location in which one might suspect an Old Norse origin, but to date one has not been forthcoming. EYETEETH, which clearly finds favour in significant if scattered areas, is in Standard English applied to the canine teeth, most particularly to those in the upper jaw directly beneath the eye, so that it is curious to find non-standard speakers quite definitely applying it to molars. JACKTEETH, recorded by Wright in his *Dialect Dictionary* in West Cornwall, is surprising in view of the standard use of JACK to refer to something such as the jack in a game of bowls, which is of *smaller* than usual size. Other non-standard words recorded as meaning MOLARS, many of them descriptive, include CHEWERS, CHOP-TEETH, DOUBLE-KNAPPERS, HOLLOW-TEETH, MOLE-TEETH, MUMMERS, MUSHERS, and TUCKS.

# ACTIVE

90

MAP 45
# ACTIVE

Besides those shown on the map, other single dialect adjectives meaning ACTIVE include BOISTEROUS in Kent, BOTHERSOME in the Isle of Man, BRAVE in Dorset, FRIM in Leicestershire, LITTY or UPSTRIGOLOUS in Somerset, PERT in Sussex, SHARP in Warwickshire, WAKEN in Yorkshire, and WIGGY-ARSED in Wiltshire. Phrases used to describe an active child include FULL OF GANNING ON in Northumberland, FULL OF VIM in Middlesex, ON THE FIDGET(S) in Yorkshire, Lincolnshire, and Essex, and ON THE ROUK or ON THE WANDER in Yorkshire, while the child is said to be a RADDLE-HEAD and a RAKE in Buckinghamshire, a RIVING LITTLE LUBBER in Yorkshire, or a TEAR-DOWN in Lincolnshire. The wide variety and often humorous nature of these descriptions is typical of the invention with which an affectionate subject is often approached by speakers of non-standard dialect.

WICK is a form of *quick*, and the full import of the non-standard word is that of being 'alive' rather than of indicating rapid movement. In confirmation of this, the expression DEAD OR WICK, that is 'dead or alive', has been recorded in County Durham. Wright (*Dialect Grammar*, para. 241) records the **w**- form of QUICK as far south as Northamptonshire. He also records examples of (-)**w**- in place of (-)**kw**- in other words such as QUART, QUIET, and SQUEAMISH, mainly in the North and Midlands but also occasionally in such southern counties as Somerset and Dorset.

This map can usefully be compared with that for the QUICK of the fingernail (Map 19). In that map the **w**- forms cover most of Northern England and thus most of those localities where WICK 'active' occurs. There is, however, an area in Lincolnshire where WICK means 'active' but where the skin at the base of the fingernail is only the QUICK with initial **kw**-.

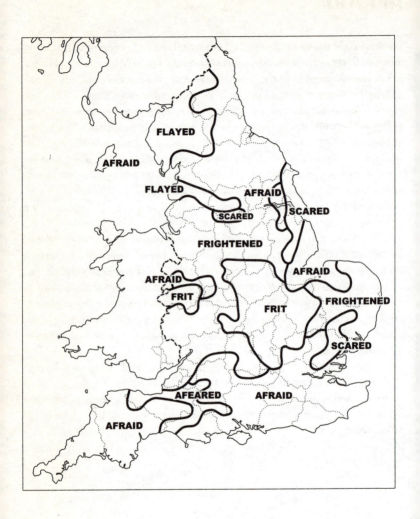

MAP 46
# AFRAID

FRIGHTENED is the most widely used of all the words meaning 'afraid', and is found in all those areas where other words are marked on the map. It is a comparatively new word, perhaps being formed as late as the seventeenth century, although it comes from the Old English verb TO FRIGHT. FRIT is also from TO FRIGHT—it is an old past participle of that verb—and it was probably in use long before the early nineteenth century when it is first recorded (compare the standard adjective LIT, from TO LIGHT). Recently it was the cause of much comment when used in the House of Commons by a prominent British politician! A number of similar words have been recorded which have not been mapped, such as FRECKENED in Lancashire and the Isle of Man, FRITTED in Rutland, and FRITTEN in Shropshire.

The oldest English word is AFEARED. Although it appears to be closely related to AFEARED, AFRAID is in fact a word which was introduced into Middle English by the Normans. AFRAINT, recorded in Wiltshire, is a similar word which has not been mapped.

Two words on the map, FLAYED and SCARED, have Old Norse origins. FLAYED, sometimes spelt FLEYED, is connected with the verb TO FLY: TO FLAY once had the meaning 'to put to flight' (that is, 'to frighten away'). Some words used to describe the effigy put in fields to frighten birds away make particular use of these terms: the standard word for this is SCARECROW, whilst it is popularly referred to in Northern England as a FLAY-CROW or a FLAY-BOGGLE (in which the second part is a form of the word BOGEY).

Some other non-standard usages recorded for AFRAID can in large measure be explained by reference to the *Shorter Oxford English Dictionary*. DUBEROUS, found in Berkshire, is recorded in the dictionary as a jocular or dialectal word meaning 'dubious, doubtful, unsure'. GALLIED, a word from Dorset, is formed from GALLY 'to frighten'. The dictionary notes this as a dialect or whaling term which was first recorded in the seventeenth century but which probably has an Old English ancestor. In the form GALLOW it is used by Shakespeare in *King Lear*. GLIFFED, from Northumberland, is clearly connected with GLIFF 'a sudden fright' and 'to frighten', Scottish and Northern English words first recorded in the mid-eighteenth and early nineteenth centuries respectively.

# SILLY

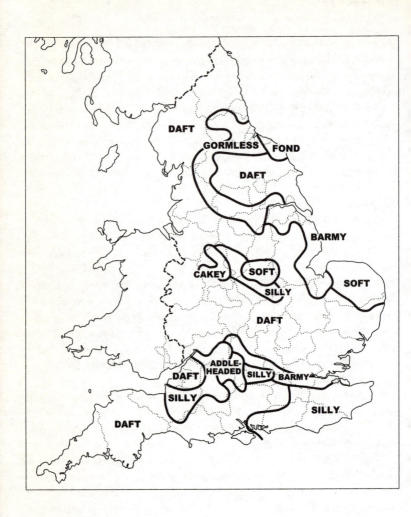

MAP 47
# SILLY

As with physical attributes such as bow legs, knock-knees, or crossed eyes (see for example Maps 49 to 51), mental states or aspects of personality provide fertile ground for the invention of non-standard dialect words. In addition to those mapped, words describing a silly person include BATCHY, BATTY, CRACKED, CRACKERS, CRANKY, DAFFY, DAPPY, DATELESS, DIBBY, DOTTY, KIMIT, LOONY, LOOPY, MAZED, NODDY, NOGGEN, NUTTY, POTTY, PUDDLED, ROOKY, TOUCHED, and WAPPY. More forcefully, someone who is stupid may be DINGY, DORMANT, DUMMEL, GOOKY, PUGGLED, STAUPS, or a DOAK, a DULBERT, a DOUGH-BAKE, or a TOOL. On the alliteration found in such lists, see BLISTER (Map 54).

The standard word SILLY began its existence in Middle English meaning 'deserving compassion or sympathy', and as a variant of the less well-known SEELY is ultimately connected with an Old English word *selig*, 'fortunate, blessed by God', the development of the modern sense being through ideas of piety, innocence, and ultimately defencelessness and vulnerability. The word acquired its modern meaning by the sixteenth century. DAFT has undergone semantic shift in much the same way, moving from meaning 'meek, humble' in Old and Middle English to its present sense, which it acquired late in the Middle English period. In contrast to DAFT and SILLY, FOND, which has now developed a standard meaning implying affection, is used here with one of its earliest meanings, dating from Middle English times.

ADDLED, originally applied to rotten eggs, has meant 'muddled' since the late fifteenth century. Keeping a food-related theme, BARMY referred originally to *barm* or yeast which creates a froth on beer, the behaviour of a silly person coming by the sixteenth century to be likened to the insubstantial frothy 'head' on a drink. The linguistic significance of the other food-related word, CAKEY, remains open to speculation.

GORMLESS, sometimes spelt GAUMLESS, is a word well known beyond its Northern England base. GORM (or GAUM), the stem of the word, is derived from Old Norse *gaumr*, 'care, heed': with the ***ending***, -LESS, added, the resulting eighteenth-century compound GORMLESS developed, meaning 'lacking in attention or understanding'.

MAP 48

# ONLY (nothing more than, merely) a child

The competing dialectal forms shown in this map are all of much the same antiquity, although one form, ONLY, has become standard. Whilst there is no precise historical evidence for the assertion, it is likely that the location of the non-standard forms in areas well removed from the South-east point to the early preference for ONLY in the area around and immediately to the north of London from which Standard English principally derives. Standard English being the synecdochic dialect by which all others are judged, it is not surprising that NOUGHT BUT and NOBBUT have become peripheral both geographically and socially.

ONLY is an Old English word made up from two other elements which have also survived into the English of today, ONE, and -LY, the suffix added to words to indicate 'characteristic of, having the qualities of'.

It is debatable whether NOUGHT BUT should in fact be written NAUGHT BUT, both NOUGHT and NAUGHT being forms with recognizable Old English pedigrees and the two seemingly having been used interchangeably for a long time. Although the two words seem to have somewhat different origins, their *-ou-* and *-au-* have generally been thought of as differences in spelling: it is interesting to notice that there are two words, NAUGHTY and NOUGHTY, meaning 'bad', 'wicked', which can be similarly compared and contrasted. The adverbs NAUGHT and NOUGHT remained in use in Standard, though somewhat literary, English until well into the nineteenth century.

NOBBUT is of somewhat questionable derivation. The *Shorter Oxford English Dictionary*, tracing its use as a word meaning 'only' to the Middle English period, considers it to be the result of a compounding of NO and BUT. An alternative explanation is that NOBBUT is a shortened form of NOUGHT (NAUGHT) BUT, since over time speakers can be expected to run together words which are habitually linked and to pronounce them in the most economical way possible.

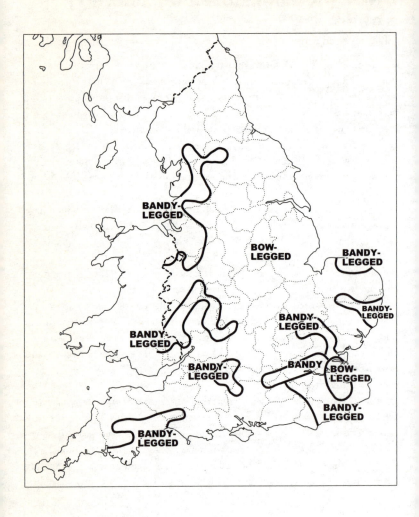

MAP 49
# BOW-LEGGED

The scattered nature of the areas of the country in which BANDY(-LEGGED) is found suggests that this description was once more widely used and that its range has decreased in the face of a more popular and somewhat more standard BOW-LEGGED. It is recorded in use from the late seventeenth century, but if it was ever itself a standard term it should now be considered to be more colloquial than BOW-LEGGED. Whilst the -LEGGED part of the compound word is, except in the South of England, almost invariably pronounced **legd** in BOW-LEGGED, it is frequently pronounced **legid** in BANDY-LEGGED.

Other words for bow-legged are BANDY-KNEED in Shropshire, BOWDY-LEGGED in Yorkshire and Kent, STRADDLY-BANDY also in Kent, BOWER-LEGGED in Cheshire, BOW-FOOTED in Northamptonshire, and SCROD-LEGGED in Somerset.

Descriptions of physical characteristics provide fertile ground for the inventive speaker of non-standard English, as study of the map for KNOCK-KNEED (Map 50) will also show. Terms descriptive of a person having feet which turn inwards or outwards, that is synonyms of PIGEON-TOED and SPLAY-FOOTED, are even more numerous. Among words descriptive of being pigeon-toed are CLEEKY-FEET, KEB-FOOTED, PINCER-TOED, PUMBLE-FOOTED, TIMBER-TOED, TOSIE, TROLL-FOOTED, TWANG-TOED, and TWILLY-TOED. Words descriptive of being splay-footed include (from a very long list) BROAD-ARROWED, PASTY-FOOTED, SHOVEL-FOOTED, SLY-FOOTED, SPLAWDERED, SPROG-HOCKED, WEB- or WEM-FOOTED, and WEDNESDAY-AND-THURSDAY, while a person with splayed feet is a DEW-DASHER in Lincolnshire and a DEW-SWEEPER in Norfolk.

# KNOCK-KNEED

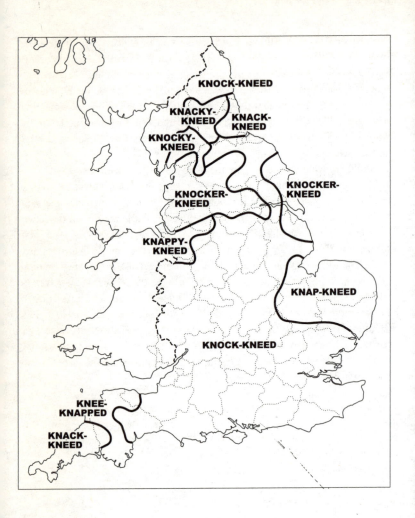

MAP 50

# KNOCK-KNEED

KNOCK-KNEED is the dominant word here, and it is in fact found in almost all places where other words have been recorded too. Furthermore, it is of course very closely related to KNOCKER- and KNOCKY-KNEED and a little more distantly to KNACK- and KNACKY-KNEED. Nevertheless, it is interesting to note that the rather different forms with KNAP, that is KNAP-KNEED, KNAPPY-KNEED, and KNEE-KNAPPED, occupy a considerable area. That the three areas concerned are widely spaced suggests that KNAP forms were once more widespread than they now are. Although there is some mixing of the forms between the areas, with KNAP-KNEED being found in Somerset and Devon where KNEE-KNAPPED is indicated, that each area shows a marked tendency to favour a different word based on KNAP suggests that they have been isolated from one another for some considerable time.

The case of KNAP words provides a good illustration of the problem which the dialectologist has in deciding on the spelling of non-standard words. KNACK and KNOCK are both well-known everyday spellings, and English speakers are not likely to be misled by the spelling into thinking that the initial *k* should be pronounced in these words. However, KNAP is far less usually found than NAP in Standard English, and it is possible that someone reading KNAP may, quite wrongly, think that in this case the *k* should be sounded. A decision has been taken for this map to include an initial *k* in the spelling of KNAP because it is historically correct to do so: like KNACK and KNOCK, KNAP began as a word imitating the sound of things striking sharply together, and at an early stage the letter *k* would have been pronounced. Such decisions are often not easy to make, are often less than wholly satisfactory, and frequently have to be explained.

As has been pointed out in the commentary to the map for BOW-LEGGED (Map 49), dialects are rich in words describing physical characteristics. Among the more unusual words for KNOCK-KNEED which have not been mapped here are CRAB-ANKLED in Lincolnshire, HURKED UP in Warwickshire, JAY-LEGGED in Yorkshire, KAY-LEGGED in Yorkshire and Hampshire, and KNUCKLE-KNEED in Suffolk.

# CROSS-EYED

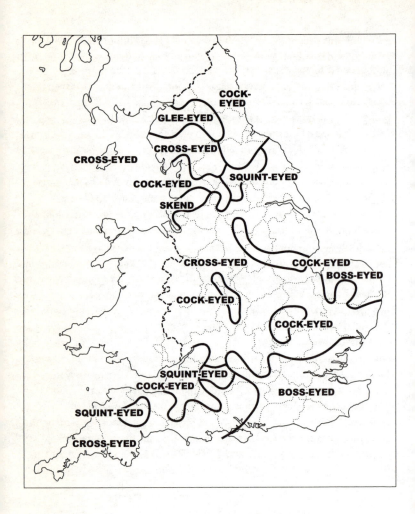

MAP 51

# CROSS-EYED

As with terms descriptive of many other physical conditions such as bow legs (Map 49) and knock-knees (Map 50), dialect synonyms for CROSS-EYED are many and display considerable inventiveness.

CROSS-EYED itself is of course purely descriptive, and is recorded from the late eighteenth century onwards. The similar-sounding COCK-EYED is recorded a little later, in the early nineteenth century, originally with the meaning relevant here relating to inward-turning eyes but a little later being extended to the general idea of crookedness or unevenness which we know in standard use today. The COCK- part of the word seems to be connected with the verb *to cock*, in Middle English meaning 'to fight' but coming to mean 'to stand up conspicuously' and then 'to lift up unevenly', as in such phrases as 'to cock one's head' or 'to cock an eyebrow'.

SQUINT-EYED is an older term, SQUINT being found referring to misaligned eyes in Middle English, sometimes in the form *asquint*. In contrast, BOSS-EYED seems to date only from the nineteenth century and always to have had a somewhat colloquial connotation: some speakers using the word regarded it as being less polite, and more modern, than CROSS-EYED. In these circumstances it is interesting that BOSS-EYED has such strong support in South-east England and East Anglia. The first element in GLEE-EYED is probably a development of *glee* in the sense of 'fun' and 'exuberance' to indicate something, in this case vision, which is out of control. This usage is echoed in Robert Burns's poem *To a Mouse*: that "The best laid schemes o' mice an' men | Gang aft a-gley". SKEND has a variant form SKENNING in Lancashire and Staffordshire.

Other terms synonymous with CROSS-EYED which are not mapped include GOG-EYED in Kent, GOGGLE-EYED in Lincolnshire, LINK-EYED in Yorkshire, and THWART-EYED in Somerset.

# GIDDY

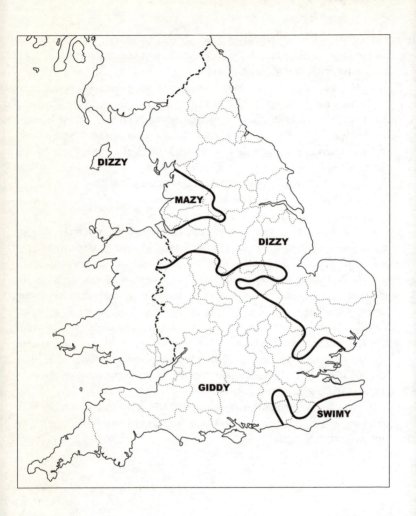

MAP 52
# GIDDY

Although both GIDDY and DIZZY are words from Old English, neither was applied to a spinning sensation in the head during the Old English period, only acquiring that meaning in Middle English. In Old English DIZZY meant 'foolish, stupid'. GIDDY had the same meaning, but could more strongly also mean 'insane, mad': according to the *Shorter Oxford English Dictionary* the root of the word in older Germanic languages is the same as GOD, its primary meaning being 'possessed by a god'.

It is not difficult to detect the origin of MAZY in the modern standard word MAZE referring to a confusing network of twisting paths. Still more relevant is the fact that in Middle English *the maze* could denote 'delirium or delusion' or 'a state of bewilderment', meanings which fit well with the notion of experiencing giddiness. MAZY itself is recorded with the present meaning in the early sixteenth century.

SWIMY is best identified through its variant form SWIMMY found in Essex and Surrey; both SWIMY and SWIMMY have also been recorded as meaning 'feeling faint' in Surrey and Sussex. *To swim* is first recorded as meaning 'to be affected with dizziness; to have a giddy sensation' in the early eighteenth century.

GIDDY is sometimes amplified to GIDDY-HEADED, DIZZY to DIZZY-HEADED, and SWIMMY to SWIMMY-HEADED. FUDDLED, a word often associated with drunkenness, has been recorded as an old word applying to general giddiness in Norfolk, and the descriptive HEAD-LIGHT and WHIRLY have been found in Cornwall and Surrey respectively. WONKY, described by the *Shorter Oxford English Dictionary* as a twentieth-century slang term, has been collected in Derbyshire: speakers of non-standard dialect are as ready as anyone to use modern slang alongside more traditional words.

# HUNGRY

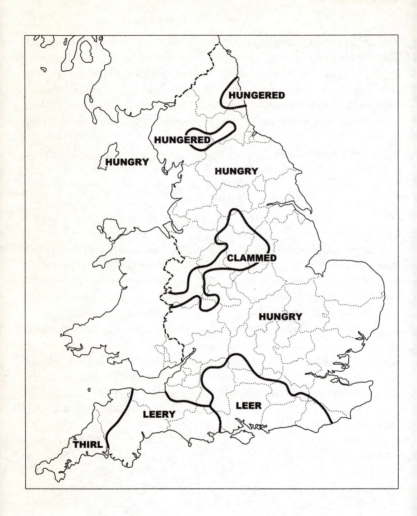

MAP 53
# HUNGRY

As Trudgill points out in *Dialects of England* (106), the distribution of words for HUNGRY illustrates the point that it is not necessarily the traditional words of southern England which have become Standard English. Although HUNGRY is found throughout the country, including those areas where other terms are shown on the map, much of the South in particular produces other words too.

HUNGRY itself is a development of an Old English word, purpose-built to indicate pain felt because of lack of food. Its variant, HUNGERED, curiously surviving in northern England, is essentially an aphetic, shortened form of an older AHUNGERED. It is marked by the *Shorter Oxford English Dictionary* as being archaic.

Whilst HUNGRY has always had its present meaning in English, LEER, which is recorded as meaning 'hungry' in the mid-nineteenth century, in Old English had the much wider, more general meaning 'empty'. The variant form LEERY is recorded by the dictionary with the meaning 'empty' from the late seventeenth century. Also of great antiquity and somewhat inventive, but like LEER and LEERY apparently lacking a long pedigree with a 'hungry' meaning, is THIRL. This in Old English meant 'a hole', and is the word which gives us the second part of NOSTRIL, which is a compound word made up of *nose* and *thirl* or '*hole*'. In its application to the emptiness associated with hunger we have a *figurative* use of the word.

CLAMMED, the other non-standard word mapped, is obscure in origin, though it may have the same Old English ancestor as CLAMP and convey the meaning of being 'gripped' by hunger. Whatever its origin it has had wide dialectal use in connection with hunger, being recorded by Wright in *The English Dialect Dictionary* in counties throughout England, and in Ireland and Wales too. The force of the word is frequently greater than HUNGRY, rather conveying the notion of 'starving': a place where animals are kept unfed before slaughter is given such non-standard dialect names as CLAMMING-HOLE, CLAMMING-HOUSE, and CLAMPEN.

As is to be expected with so basic a human experience as hunger, the dialects show a wide range of words beyond those mapped. These include FAMMELLED in Oxfordshire, GANT in Yorkshire, WALLOW in Cumberland, and YAP in Northumberland.

# BLISTER

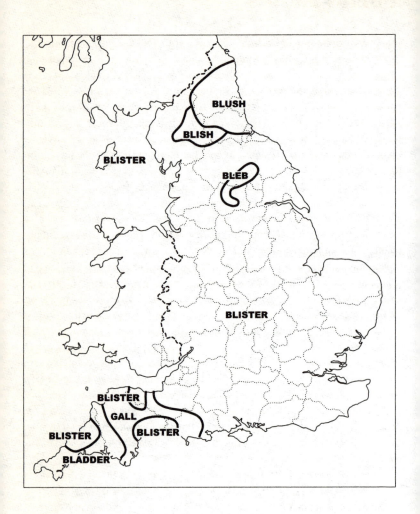

MAP 54
# a BLISTER

It is an interesting fact that many non-standard dialect **synonyms**, words which are used to represent the same thing or idea, are linked to one another by **alliteration**, the use of the same sounds as part of their construction. So, for example, several of the words used around England to describe bread or pastry that has not risen begin with a **kl-** sound: CLABBY, CLAMMY, CLEATY, CLIBBY, CLIDGY, CLINGY, CLIT, CLITTIED, CLITTY, CLOSE, CLUTCHY. So too the rung of a ladder may be called a SPELL, SPINDLE, SPOKE, STAB, STABBER, STAFF, STALE, STALL, STAP, STAVE, STAVVER, STAY, STEE-SPELL, STEE-STEP, STEP, or STOWER. To the **bl-** words mapped here, BLADDER, BLEB, BLISH, BLISTER, and BLUSH, can be added the alliterating BLASTER found in Hampshire.

Non-alliterating words for BLISTER are GALL, mapped here, and unmapped FLISH in Yorkshire and WEAL in Lincolnshire.

BLADDER and GALL are the oldest of the words for a blister shown here, both being used in Old English in that sense. Although it is now very specifically associated with something much larger than a blister, BLADDER particularly survives in modern Standard English with reference to small swellings in compounds such as BLADDERWRACK, that seaweed which has many small air sacs in its fronds. GALL, which began as a word specifically meaning a painful swelling or blister, has of course come to refer more generally to any sore place caused by rubbing or chafing. Both BLISTER and BLEB, the latter in its more usual form BLOB, are Middle English words for a blister. In the twentieth century BLEB has acquired a particular scientific meaning, 'a swelling due to injury on the surface of a cell'.

# SPLINTER

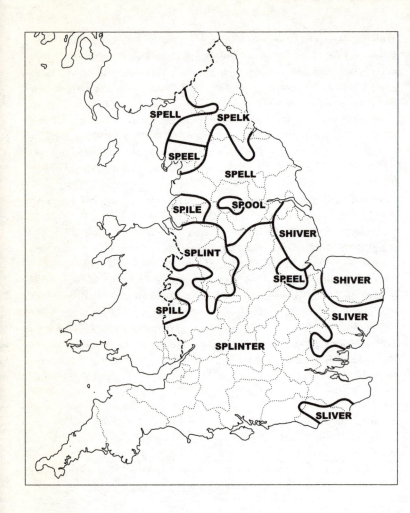

MAP 55

# a SPLINTER

With the exception of SPILE and SPOOL, all the words mapped here are recorded as having been in use referring to a tiny piece of wood in the Middle English period. Although there is no written evidence to prove it, it is probable that SHIVER and SLIVER, with Old English links, and perhaps some of the other words too, have been in use for longer.

SPLINTER itself, together with its very close relation SPLINT, entered the language from Dutch or German. SPLINTER is apparently slightly the older word in English.

The similar-sounding set SPEEL, SPELK, SPELL, and SPILL are all well attested in Middle English. However, it is likely that SPEEL and SPELK at least, with close Scandinavian parallels and geographical bases in areas of Norse settlement, have existed in England since an earlier period. SPELL also, as a probable variant of a now-obsolete word SPELD, has close associations with Norse: again the location of the word suggests its use since the Viking age.

According to the *Shorter Oxford English Dictionary*, SPILL in the sense of 'splinter' is related to SPILE, both being of Dutch or German descent, though SPILE is not recorded until the sixteenth century. Curiously, however, the dictionary records another word SPILL, of different Dutch/German origin, meaning 'spool', at once suggesting a connection between SPILL and the SPOOL which is found meaning 'splinter' in West and South Yorkshire even though there is no record of it having meant 'splinter' in the Standard English of any period. This connection between SPILL and SPOOL also leads one to suspect that the distinction between SPILL 'splinter' and SPILL 'spool' is not an absolute one: indeed, it is probable that SPEEL, SPELK, SPELL, SPILE, SPILL, and SPOOL are *cognates*, words ultimately descending from a common ancestor.

As with words for BLISTER (Map 54) and APRIL FOOL (Map 76), a remarkable feature of the dialect synonyms for SPLINTER is the element of alliteration. Of twenty-three words recorded for SPLINTER in the Survey of English Dialects, twenty begin with *s-* and fifteen of these with *sp-*.

# ACHE

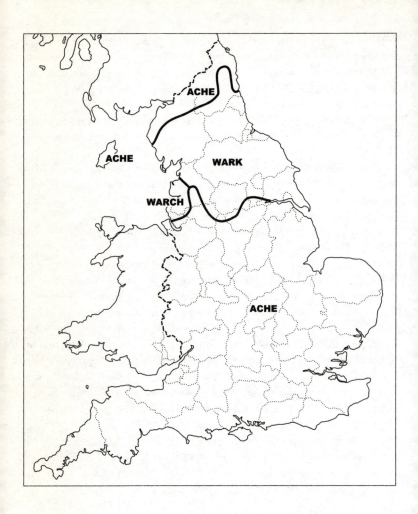

MAP 56

# to ACHE

Until the eighteenth century it was quite usual to pronounce ACHE with a **ch** sound when it was used as a noun but with today's **k** sound when it was a verb, the verb having a *k* spelling as well. Curiously, we now have the *ch* spelling but the **k** sound for both the verb and the noun, mainly because Dr Johnson wrongly thought that both were derived from Greek *akhos*, 'pain', and declared that they were "more grammatically written *ache*". Wright (*Dialect Grammar*, para. 340) states that the **ch** pronunciation of ACHE was to be found in the dialects of Cheshire, Shropshire, and Staffordshire, but there is no evidence that it remains in any non-standard dialects now.

ACHE is descended from the Old English verb *acan* and noun *æce*. WARK and WARCH derive from a parallel Old English noun *wærc* and its Old Norse counterpart *verkr*. It is not surprising to find WARK dominant over much of the North, as, with its final **k** sound, it has a strong echo of the Norse form, whereas the final *c* of the Old English word, representing a **ch** sound, is seen to survive in Lancashire and Merseyside, which were not heavily settled by Vikings. This distinction between a 'soft' Old English sound and a 'hard' Old Norse sound is that which can be seen in the contrast between FLITCH and FLICK (Map 66), BRIDGE and BRIG (Map 71).

WARCH and WARK are closely related to the word WORK, all having the same Germanic root. Indeed, WORK is recorded by the *Shorter Oxford English Dictionary* meaning 'to ache' from the late Middle English period, and may still occasionally be heard with this meaning today.

# FESTER

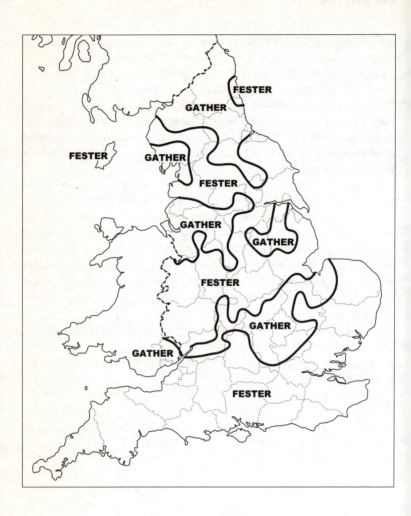

MAP 57

# to FESTER

A comparison of the words FESTER and GATHER provides an excellent example of the often-occurring situation in which a newer English word has become standard and has gained popularity at the expense of the older, and yet in which that older form has retained a remarkable hold in the non-standard dialects.

FESTER is the well-known word describing what a wound does when left untreated. Deriving from Old French, it is one of very many words which entered English in the Middle English period. It is not surprising to see it as the normal usage of traditional speakers throughout southern England and East Anglia, and to see it well established too in large areas of the Midlands and the North. The small FESTER enclave on the coast in the North-east testifies to the powerful influence of urbanization and coastal movement in the transmission of new linguistic forms, influences which are also to be seen in other maps such as that for BRIDGE (Map 71).

Although it is now eclipsed in the standard dialect, GATHER long predates FESTER: the *Shorter Oxford English Dictionary* records it as having an Old English meaning 'accumulate and come to a head; develop a purulent swelling', precisely the meaning required here. The large yet scattered areas of distribution of GATHER today suggest that its popularity, although lessening, has been slow to diminish. Most remarkable is the large band of its distribution across central southern England from the Severn to the Wash, which encompasses an area that has been under strong Standard English influence for many centuries. Something of the continuing power of the Old English word is suggested by its use in the dictionary definition of FESTER: 'Of a wound or sore: gather or produce pus.'

Amongst other unmapped non-standard words recorded for FESTER are BEAL (related to *boil*) in Northumberland, CANKER in Norfolk, DAG and MATTER in Yorkshire, and RANGLE in Herefordshire.

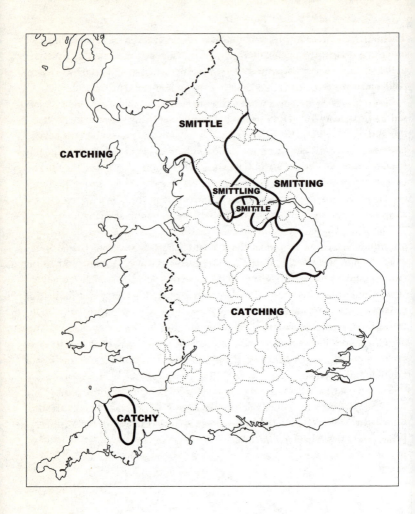

MAP 58

# INFECTIOUS

The most widely used word describing an infectious illness is French-derived CATCHING, demonstrating as so often happens that words entering the language in the Middle English period through Anglo-Norman had great power to supplant older words.

CATCH has, and has had, a wide range of meanings, beginning with an early sense of 'to chase' and for long including modern notions concerned with capture and snatching. Its use to mean 'take by infection', and the use of the adjective CATCHING, are recorded in late Middle English. Given the non-standard speaker's tendency to create new versions of existing words, the variant form CATCHY is not surprising as a less standard form of CATCHING, though it is interesting to see that its use, apart from an isolated occurrence in one locality in Yorkshire, is concentrated in Devon, where it has been recorded in five villages.

The three words beginning with SMIT-, namely SMITTING, SMITTLE, and SMITTLING, are all related and can be regarded as variants of the same ultimate word, though again it can be seen that local preference for particular forms is strong. The Old English word from which all are descended was *smitte*, meaning 'spot, stain, smear': the *Shorter Oxford English Dictionary* records this, as SMIT, meaning 'infection, contagion' in Scotland and the North in the early nineteenth century, but refers also to an Old English verb, *smittian*, which meant 'infect, affect by contagion', so that the connection of SMIT with disease is clearly very early. Ultimately related to SMIT(-) words are others such as BESMIRCH, SMITE, SMUDGE, and SMUT.

Besides the words mapped, non-standard speakers also say CAPTIOUS, CONTAGIOUS, INFECTING, INFECTIOUS, INFECTIVE, LATCHING, and TAKING. Use of CONTAGIOUS and INFECTIOUS, the latter of which is very widely known, illustrates the point that non-standard speakers can normally be expected to have access to a number of different styles of speech and are quite able to use Standard English words when they judge them to be appropriate.

# ADDER

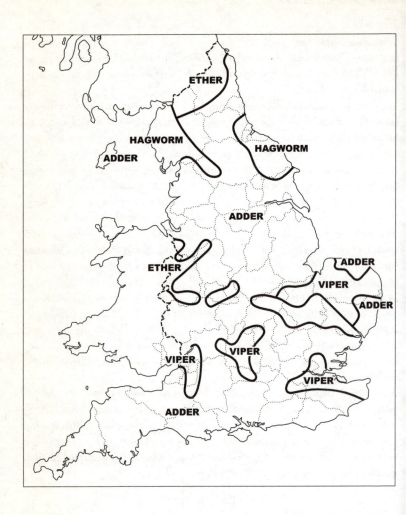

MAP 59

# ADDER

As this map shows, the Old English-derived word ADDER has remained in widespread use, whilst the French-derived VIPER, which was introduced in the Middle English period, has a very restricted and patchy distribution. ADDER is also frequently used in those areas where VIPER is found. ETHER, which rhymes with *heather*, is a variant form of ADDER. The strong survival of Old English words for which there are French-derived alternatives is most to be expected when they have 'domestic' or 'everyday' referents such as routine activities or familiar objects.

ADDER is one of a small group of English words beginning with **a** which once began with **n**. The Old English form of the word was *nædre,* which in Middle English became *naddre.* In the fourteenth and fifteenth centuries *a naddre* came increasingly to be divided instead as *an addre*, resulting ultimately in the word we have today. Other words which have undergone the same development include APRON (earlier *naperon*) and AUGER (earlier *nafogar*). See also the map for AUNT(IE) (Map 4). Reinterpretation of the boundaries between words is known technically as *metanalysis*.

The -WORM part of HAGWORM derives from Old English *wyrm* and Old Norse *ormr*, meaning 'snake, serpent, dragon', and both influences are no doubt present when the word refers to an earthworm. In HAGWORM it is probable that the Norse influence predominates, since the word is seen to be found in areas of Viking settlement. (Norse influence is also to be seen in the names of landmarks such as the Great Orm at Llandudno and Worms Head on Gower, both on the Welsh coast along which Vikings raided and settled.) HAG- is connected either with a word referring to wet moorland or with another referring to woodland, both of which are Norse derived.

There are areas in the Midlands and East Anglia where no word for ADDER was recorded. It is likely that these are areas in which the adder is less commonly found than elsewhere.

# FEMALE CAT

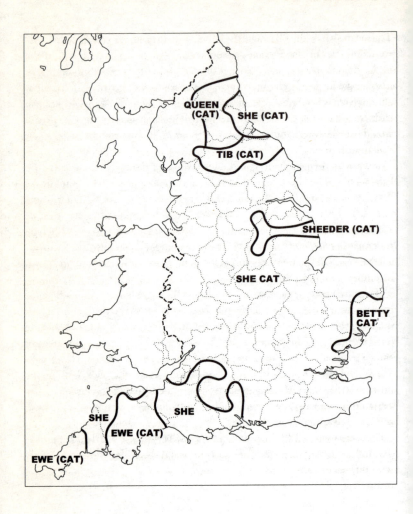

MAP 60

# FEMALE CAT

The headword or reference word by which the female cat is referred to in the Survey of English Dialects is TABBY-CAT, suggesting that the originators of the Survey expected to find many speakers using that word. In fact, as can be seen from this map, TABBY-CAT was not a usual response given by non-standard dialect speakers, although it has been recorded referring to a female cat in Northumberland, Lancashire, and the Isle of Man. Nor is it likely that many standard dialect speakers would use the word in this context, since TABBY, although commonly used in the description of cats, normally refers to their colour rather than to their gender. The word, deriving from the name of a district of Baghdad, was first used in English late in the sixteenth century to refer to a type of striped fabric first made in that city. It came to be used as a description of striped cats around half a century later.

In spite of the usual connection of TABBY with colour, however, the *Shorter Oxford English Dictionary* notes that TABBY CAT has sometimes been used to refer to a female cat, or even more generally to any domestic cat. TABBY itself has at various times acquired a variety of extended meanings such as 'an elderly spinster' and 'an attractive young woman', the connection of which with the original and modern meanings is quite obscure.

Women's names, or words describing women, seem often to have been applied to cats. TIB, which is seen to be used over a wide area of North Yorkshire, is shown by the dictionary to have a variety of meanings, frequently used in the sixteenth and seventeenth centuries, ranging from any working-class woman, through girlfriend or sweetheart, to a promiscuous woman or prostitute. Perhaps a diminutive form of ISABEL, TIB has itself sometimes been used as a proper name, and it can be seen that another abbreviated proper name, BETTY, refers to a she-cat in East Anglia, while its close relation BESS-CAT has been collected in Durham. Two other female names, JENNY and the well-known MOGGY (a variation of MAGGIE), occur as dialect words for the female cat in Yorkshire and Norfolk respectively.

# FLEA

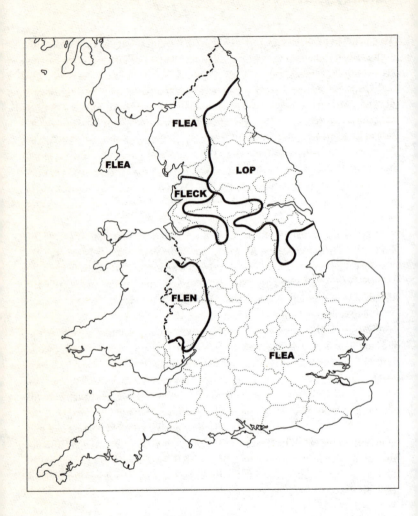

MAP 61

# FLEA

This map is one of several in which the distribution of words reflects the predominance of Anglo-Saxon or Viking peoples in different areas of England, since FLEA is an Old English word and LOP is from Old Norse. However, unlike such maps as those for ACHE (Map 56) or BEAK (Map 64), that for FLEA shows the Norse-derived word on one side of Northern England only. Although there was probably considerable mingling of different groups, Viking settlement on the eastern side of England was predominantly by invaders from Denmark whilst that in the North-west and in various other places on the western side of Britain was largely from Norway. It is tempting to suppose therefore that LOP was a word favoured by Danes, and that Norwegians preferred the Norse equivalent of FLEA, *fló*. It may simply be, however, that FLEA is so strongly established that it has eroded a LOP area which once extended from its present base to the west coast.

LOP, together with a variant LOPPERD recorded in Yorkshire, is in origin a very expressive word, since its base is the Old Norse verb *hlaupa*, 'to leap', this reasonably being adapted to apply to the jumping insect. English equivalents of this very basic kind of naming are JUMPER in Essex and, descriptive of the flea's size, MIDGEN in the Isle of Man and MIDGET in Berkshire.

In spite of the existence of a very strong LOP area, FLEA is by far the more dominant word. It is found in all the English counties, and the other words mapped, FLECK and FLEN, are derivatives of it. FLECK is interesting in that its final **k** sound is a direct descendant of an Old English form. FLEA in Old English was either *fléa* or *fléah*. The *h* of the second form represented a sound similar to *ch* in Scots *loch*, and this guttural sound has survived as the ending of the word FLECK seen here. FLEN probably represents a plural form, showing the *-en* ending of such words as *children* and *oxen*: it is certainly used as a plural in the three counties for which it is recorded, Shropshire, Herefordshire, and Worcestershire, but all three also provide evidence of a plural form FLENS which suggests that FLEN is thought of as a singular too. Other FLEA-words are FLAYTH, recorded as a plural form in Lancashire, FLEFF in Lancashire, Cheshire, and Staffordshire, and probably the curious plural FYOFF in Shropshire.

# HEDGEHOG

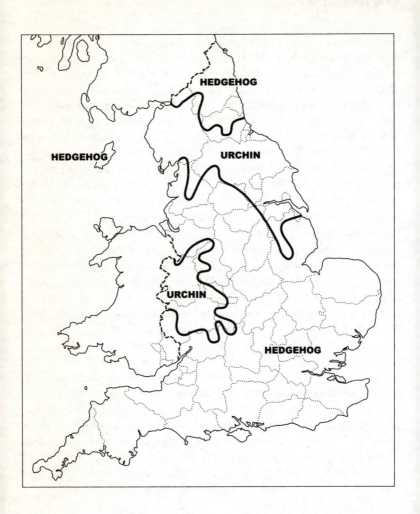

MAP 62

# HEDGEHOG

HEDGEHOG is an obvious English compound (HEDGE + HOG 'pig') and URCHIN is derived from French, but both words are first recorded in use in the Middle English period.

The HOG element of HEDGEHOG may be one of the few words borrowed from the British Celtic inhabitants by the Anglo-Saxons when they invaded Britain, but it is more likely to be purely English. (More certain candidates in a surprisingly small list of Celtic borrowings include BROCK 'badger', and the name AVON, from *afon*, 'river'.) The fact that both HOG and HEDGE are found in Old English suggests that HEDGEHOG existed as an animal name before the Norman conquest but that it is simply not to be found in any written records.

URCHIN derives from the Old Norman French word *herichon*, which is itself a descendant of the Latin word for hedgehog, *hericius*. Application to the hedgehog is the earliest use of the word: it does not seem to have been applied to a mischievous child until later in the Middle English period, and only came to denote a poor, ragged child in the sixteenth century. However, apparently because the word is now commonly thought to apply only to children, the non-standard dialect animal-term is frequently prefaced with such descriptive words as PRICKLY-, PRICKY-, and PRICKLY-BACKED-. In spite of the fact that it is probably declining as a non-standard word for the hedgehog, URCHIN retains a reasonably strong presence, and in SEA-URCHIN it has survived relating to a spiny creature in Standard English too.

Variations on HEDGEHOG are HEDGEPIG, used by Shakespeare in *Macbeth* and found in Oxfordshire and Berkshire, and HEDGY-BOAR, collected in Devon. PRICKLY- is used as a preface to PIG in Yorkshire, and the HEDGE- element is replaced by FURZE- (or possibly FUZZ-) to give FURZEPIG (FUZZPIG) in Devon.

MAP 63

# PIGEONS

The standard word PIGEON is easy to locate in a dictionary and can readily be explained as descending from the Old French word for a young bird, *pijon*. QUIST, on the other hand, is an excellent example of a word which, written in that form to reflect the pronunciation given to it by its users, cannot easily be located in a general dictionary. Non-standard words are often of this kind, requiring effort to unearth information about them.

A reasonable strategy when faced with a word which is not listed in a dictionary is to imagine other ways in which that word might be spelt. Although QUIST is not to be found in the *Shorter Oxford English Dictionary*, the similar QUEEST *is* listed as a word of late medieval origin meaning 'the woodpigeon'. It is labelled 'obsolete except dialectal', and reference is made to another dialectal 'woodpigeon' word WOODQUEST. Most importantly, the word is said to be an alteration of CUSHAT, which the dictionary states is from Old English and chiefly used in Scots and northern English, though ultimately of obscure origin. The more detailed *Oxford English Dictionary* goes to some length to discuss the possible origins of CUSHAT, which it identifies as Old English *cuscote*, a compound made up of two parts *cu-* and *-scote*. The first element has variously been seen as imitating the pigeon's call or as a survival of an Old English word meaning 'pure, modest'. The second element may be related to SHOOT in its sense of 'darting, rapid movement'. All this is, however, conjectural, as is much non-standard dialect etymologizing.

Although unknown to general dictionaries, QUIST is well recorded in the *English Dialect Dictionary*, where it is listed with wide distribution and forms which include QUEEST and also QUEECE, QUEEZE, and QUEST. CUSHAT is shown to have a wide distribution too, especially in the North and Midlands, and versions which include COWSHOT, COWSORT, and CUSHY. Reference is usually to the woodpigeon, though the words are sometimes applied to other related pigeons and doves: the QUIST mapped here sometimes refers to wild pigeons, especially on the edge of the mapped area. As a dialect synonym for PIGEONS, QUIST is clearly a ***collective plural*** as well as a singular, but some speakers consider it to be singular only and refer to pigeons collectively as QUISTS.

MAP 64
# BEAK

BEAK is the newest of the words mapped here, having come into Middle English from Old French. Although BILL is comparatively little used now, it is likely that it was the most widely used English form before the introduction of BEAK: as the map shows, even today BILL is to be found in places as far apart as Northumberland and Cornwall. The spread of BEAK is an example of the way in which a new word can become dominant, eroding the position held by a previously well-established term.

Unlike the particularly English BILL and the decidedly French-derived BEAK, NEB has its roots in two different, albeit closely related, languages, Old English and Old Norse. Although there was an Old English word *nebb* from which the modern word has descended, the distribution of NEB in the North and East of England, the areas of Viking settlement, leads one to the conclusion that the influence of the Old Norse version of the word, *nef*, must have played a part in its remarkably strong survival in the face of the supremacy of BEAK. Interesting uses of NEB today include the verb NEB meaning 'to gossip', and the description of a design of clogs with a narrow front projection as being DUCK-NEBBED.

A beak is also called a CRUP in the Isle of Man, a PECKER in Somerset, Wiltshire, and Dorset, and a PICK in Shropshire. PECKER is self-explanatory, whilst the origin of CRUP is obscure. PICK of course sounds rather like BEAK, and is probably very strongly influenced by it, but there are also various implements such as the pickaxe whose action in use imitates the beak of a bird, and association with such tools is likely to have affected the speaker's usage. The interaction of two or more influences in this way can often lead to the creation of a new word or usage, especially in non-standard speech.

# PUPPY

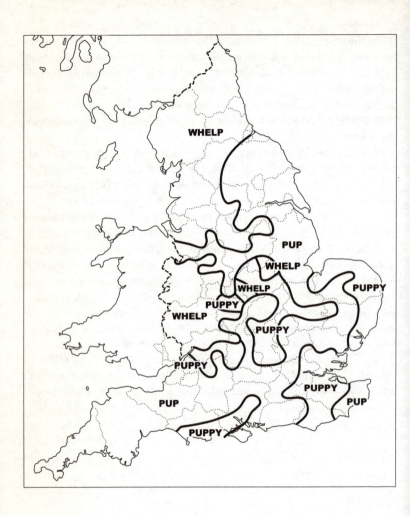

MAP 65
# PUPPY

The essential distinction in non-standard choice of words for a young dog is that between the Old English word WHELP and the medieval French import PUPPY. As is frequently to be seen in such situations, the earlier English word has retained support in areas away from the centre of much linguistic innovation in the Southeast: in this case that support has been substantial.

The Old English spelling of WHELP is *hwelp*, indicating most clearly that it was pronounced with an initial **hw** sound, as were other words today spelt with *wh-* such as the pronoun and determiner WHICH, the **adverb** and **conjunction** WHEN, and the verb TO WHET. In Old English the **h** in **hw-** was a forceful guttural sound like the **ch** in modern Scots LOCH. In the Middle English period words which had been spelt with *hw-* in Old English came to be spelt with *wh-* in Midland and southern England but with such combinations as *qu-*, *qv-*, and *qw-* in northern and especially Scottish dialects, indicating that the harsh sound was being kept in the north but lessened further south (Joseph and Elizabeth Wright, *Middle English Grammar*, paras. 300, 303). The subsequent development has been that the **h-** has been dropped entirely from most English speech, and that the guttural has been 'softened' in those areas where it held on longest, resulting in the **hw-** pronunciation which, as mentioned in the commentary for QUICK (Map 19), is still a distinctive feature of modern Scots pronunciation.

PUPPY is first found in English records in the fifteenth century when, true to its derivation from Old French *popée*, 'doll', it denoted a small 'toy' dog kept as the plaything of a wealthy lady. This meaning remained in English until the seventeenth century, by which time the word had acquired its modern meaning too. PUP is derived from PUPPY by **back-formation**, the process which gives us BEG, BURGLE, ENTHUSE, LIAISE, and SLEAZE from, respectively, BEGGAR, BURGLAR, ENTHUSIASM, LIAISON, and SLEAZY, and the curious verb TO BUTTLE from BUTLER. In the case of PUP(PY), the *-y* ending has apparently been identified as a **diminutive suffix**, a word-ending indicating smallness (or familiarity), as in DOGGY or DADDY, with PUP being constructed in consequence as the base word from which PUPPY was thought to come.

# FLITCH

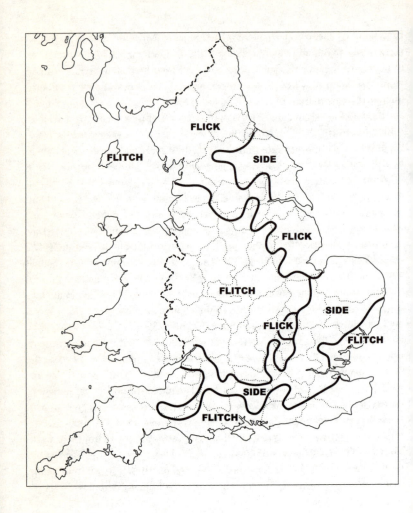

MAP 66
# FLITCH (of bacon)

In its contrast between the 'soft' **ch** sound in FLITCH and the 'hard' **k** sound in FLICK this map can be compared with that for BRIDGE (Map 71), where the sound in BRIDGE contrasts with that in BRIG, or, with even more relevance, with the WARCH/WARK distinction in the ACHE map (Map 56). In each case the essential distinction is between the Old English soft sound and the Old Norse hard sound, and the distributions of the words thus created reflects the settlement patterns resulting from the Viking invasions: Norse-speaking settlers strongly influenced the dialects of Northern and Eastern England, whilst the influence of the earlier English inhabitants is strongest in the Midlands and Southern England.

The words FLITCH and FLICK originally applied to the salted and cured side of any meat-producing animal. Now, however, they have a very specific meaning, applying only to a side of bacon. Strictly speaking, therefore, the gloss 'OF BACON' which is appended to these terms by some speakers is now redundant. This is not so for SIDE, which as well as being synonymous with FLITCH and FLICK can refer to other meat (SIDE OF BEEF, OF LAMB, and so on). It is therefore not surprising that SIDE is more frequently glossed 'OF BACON' than the other terms.

In the origins of meat terms we can see something of medieval social history. It has often been observed that whilst the animal names BULLOCK, SHEEP, and PIG are English words, terms for the meat which they provide, BEEF, MUTTON, and PORK, derive from the French, and that this reflects the origins of the people who, respectively, tended the animals and ate the meat. This observation can be refined. Meat of lower quality is likely to have an English-derived name: BREAST, HEART, OX LIVER, PIG'S HEAD, OFFAL. Better-quality meat generally has a French-derived name: LOIN, SIRLOIN, RUMP, CHINE. It is not surprising to find in FLITCH, FLICK, and SIDE terms which predate French influence on the language, since they relate to large pieces of meat requiring further preparation before being consumed. Although the picture is complicated by many social, historical, and random factors, meat terminology clearly reflects the fact that Norman households in the Middle Ages kept to themselves most available meat, and that of the better quality, while English speakers raised the animals, prepared the food, and ate less well.

# GOOSEBERRY

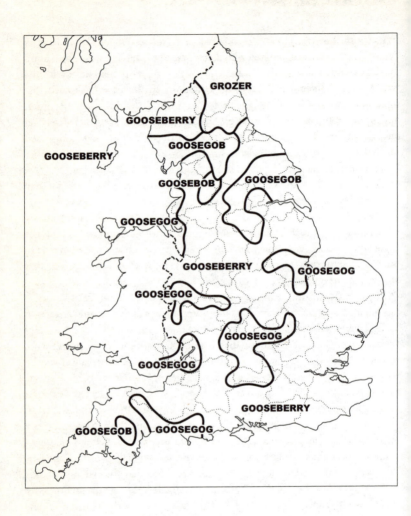

MAP 67

# GOOSEBERRY

The origin of the word GOOSEBERRY is obscure, but the *Shorter Oxford English Dictionary* suggests that the answer may lie with GROZER, the synonym which is seen to be used in extreme North-east England. GROZER is clearly a form of the French dialectal word *groser*, descended from Old French *groseille*, and the dictionary suggests that it is this which has given rise to the English word GOOSE-BERRY, first recorded in use in the sixteenth century. Scottish cultural links with France remained strong particularly up to the time of Scottish union with England in the eighteenth century, and it is interesting to note the existence of a non-standard word which is essentially French continuing in use on the Scottish border.

If the dictionary is correct in its suggestion that the first part of GOOSEBERRY derives from GROZER, it is not hard to imagine how a form such as GROZER-BERRY, seeming alien to most English speakers, could readily become the more English-sounding GOOSEBERRY away from the area of strongest continuing French influence. The tendency for speakers to substitute familiar words for alien-sounding ones, often endowing the substitute with an erroneous but apparently legitimate explanation by a process of folk etymology, is what has led ASPARAGUS to become SPARROW-GRASS for some non-standard speakers, or MOLARS to be renamed MAULERS (Map 44).

GOOSEGOG, which many English speakers beyond the area for which it is mapped probably know as a colloquial and perhaps childish version of GOOSE-BERRY, is the best known of the remaining words. The dictionary records its first use in the early nineteenth century, and takes the -GOG element to be an alteration of GOB in the Middle English and dialectal sense of 'a mass, a lump'. BOB too has various similar meanings, including 'a bunch, a cluster', used first in Middle English and now regarded as Scots and northern English. GOOSEGOG, GOOSEGOB, and GOOSEBOB therefore appear to be related, building on the GOOSE- element and translating as 'goose-lump'.

# GORSE

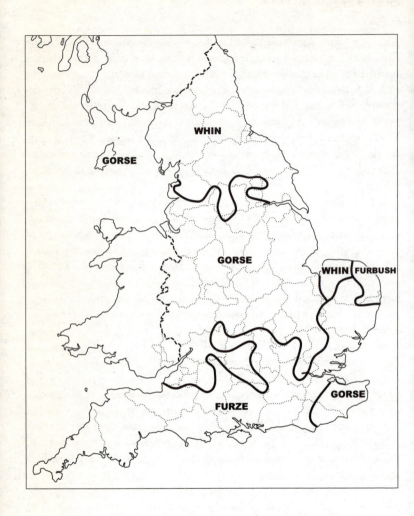

MAP 68

# GORSE

Determining which of several synonyms is the standard can be a problem for the lexicographer when, as in the case of FURZE, GORSE, and WHIN, alternatives are presented, none of which is deemed to warrant a 'dialectal' label and only one of which, WHIN, is marked for dominant regional, in this case Scottish and Northern, bias. The *Shorter Oxford English Dictionary* takes GORSE to be the word by which the other two are defined, and in view of its familiarity it is perhaps reasonable to assume that GORSE would be regarded by many as the standard word for the spiny yellow-flowered plant which all three words denote. However, the fact that WHIN and FURZE occupy a considerable amount of territory indicates the general principle that one must be careful when determining what terms are likely to be most well known to native English speakers.

Both FURZE and GORSE are attested in Old English, respectively as *fyrs* and *gors* or *gorst*. The ultimate origin of FURZE is unknown. GORSE, however, can be traced to the Indo-European parent family, where its ancestor seems to have meant 'rough' or 'prickly'. There are closely related words in both Latin and Old High German meaning 'barley' which, though less prickly than gorse, has long bristles, or *awns*, projecting from it. FURBUSH, along with a similar Norfolk term FURRA-BUSH, is doubtless a version of FURZE.

The dictionary, marking WHIN for chiefly North-British use and as appearing first in late Middle English, speculates that it may ultimately be of Scandinavian origin, and cites similar words in Swedish, Danish, and Norwegian relating to grasses. Its presence in the English areas of dominant Viking settlement supports this supposition. It is probable that the small isolated WHIN area in Norfolk was once connected to the larger northern area by instances of WHIN usage in Lincolnshire which have been eroded by GORSE.

BROOM has been recorded meaning 'gorse' in Northumberland, Westmorland, Lancashire, Yorkshire, and Suffolk. In the standard dialect BROOM refers to a plant different from GORSE, but its non-standard application to various yellow-flowering plants cannot be regarded as being 'wrong'. As the eminent American dialect lexicographer Frederic Cassidy has observed, "People are annoyingly casual about the application of names".

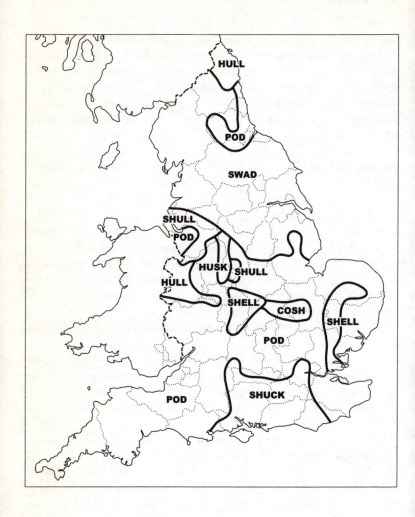

MAP 69

# pea-POD

The standard word POD, which is found throughout the country, is a curious and comparatively new word. It is derived from a long-obsolete PODWARE, which in Middle English referred to crops and animal-fodder before coming to be applied to plants which have pods. By the late seventeenth century POD had been produced by back-formation, the longer word being split to suggest, erroneously, that it had once been created by fusion of a word for the seedcase, POD, with another for the commodities or crops, WARE.

The oldest of the mapped words are SWAD and HULL. SWAD is in fact a variation on the closely related words SWARD and SWARTH, which come from parallel Old English words with meanings generally concerned with skin, rind, and outer coverings. SWARD in particular has close Old Norse connections historically, so that it is not surprising to find the similar SWAD keeping a strong presence in the areas of original Viking settlement. Today we have the familiar if rather archaic word SWADDLE, 'to wrap a child up firmly', this being closely related to the more common word SWATHE but preserving the spelling with *d* of non-standard SWAD in a Standard English word. HULL, like SWAD/SWARD/SWARTH an Old English word, was perhaps more usual than the others in the Old English period in applying to a seed-pod. The HULL of a ship may be a development of this word, though it is likely that it is at least influenced by, if not directly derived from, HOLL, 'a hollow place'.

Of the other words shown, Old English-derived SHELL is first recorded applying to a pod in late Middle English, and the obscure SHUCK appears in the late seventeenth century. SHULL seems to be a variety of SHELL influenced by HULL, with which it is closely linked geographically. The small but quite distinct area for COSH suggests that it has a firm historical origin related to a seed-pod, and its use to mean 'a heavy stick or bludgeon', or indeed a more pliable striking weapon, derives from this earlier and more innocent application.

Other words recorded include HUCK in Wiltshire and Kent, HUD in Somerset, Oxfordshire, and Berkshire, HUSK in Norfolk, POSH in Northamptonshire, and PUSKET as a special children's word in Suffolk.

# POND

MAP 70

# POND

The word POND itself, dating from Middle English times, has always specifically denoted a man-made watering place, and it is this sense which is intended in this map. The close relationship of POND with POUND, 'an enclosure', points to the fact that early ponds were often deliberately constructed to hold fish, at a time when fishponds were a vital part of the rural economy of inland areas of the country.

Apart from DUB, which like POND is Middle English, the other words mapped here, MERE, PIT, and POOL, are all known to have been in use in the Old English period. Today MERE survives particularly in place-names and is suggestive of natural lake-sized areas of standing water. Formerly, however, it denoted areas of water varying in size from a pond, as here, to the sea, and in the latter connection we can see its descent from Latin *mare*, its relationship with French *mer*, and its survival in the English word MERMAID. PIT has always suggested a hole deliberately excavated for some purpose, including for use as a pond, whereas POOL seems always to have referred principally to a small water-filled hollow which occurred naturally.

The question asked by researchers for the Survey of English Dialects in order to collect the responses shown on this map refers specifically to a water-filled place 'on a farm', the intention being to record words for an artificially-constructed pond. Another question referred to a water-filled hollow "in a field", and was designed to record words for a natural pool. The fact that there is considerable overlap between the words collected through each question points in part to the fact that the questions were perhaps worded too loosely. However, the existence of cohesive areas on this map where 'artificial' POND and PIT or 'natural' MERE and POOL (and DUB) occur as responses to the same question suggests that matters of naturalness or artificiality are of little consequence for many speakers. The basic list of words recorded for an artificial 'POND' is DAM, DEW-POND, DIP, DUB, LODGE, MERE, MOOT (compare MOAT), PIT, POOL, and POUND, and that for a natural 'POOL' is BOG-HOLE, DAM, DEW-POND, DIKE, DUB, DUM-HOLE, HOLE, HOLLAN, LODGE, MERE, PIT, POND, POUND, and STELL.

# BRIDGE

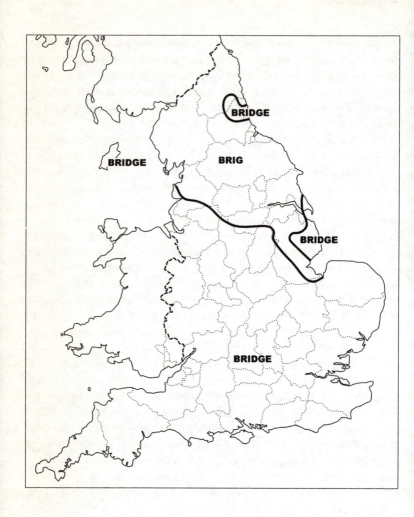

MAP 71

# BRIDGE

BRIDGE and BRIG are very closely related to one another, but their different histories mean that there is good reason for them to be considered as separate words rather than simply as different pronunciations of the same word. BRIDGE is descended from Old English *brycg*, the *-cg* spelling indicating that it ended with the 'soft' sound which we now spell with *-dge*. BRIG, however, is descended from Old Norse *bryggja* which, in the *-gg-*, contains the 'hard' sound with which the word now ends. The existence of BRIG in Northern and much of Eastern England, the main areas of Viking settlement, testifies to its Norse origin. Other 'soft'/'hard', Old English/Old Norse distinctions of this kind are to be seen in CHURCH and KIRK, SHIRT and SKIRT, the latter of course now with a difference in meaning. Compare also the map for FLITCH (Map 66), and the WARCH/WARK distinction discussed at the ACHE map (Map 56).

In Somerset and in parts of Wiltshire and Devon the pronunciation **birdge** is found. This should be regarded as a variety of the word BRIDGE in which the *-r-* has changed position with the following vowel. The movement of sounds or letters in a word in this way is known as ***metathesis***: it is the process which, in many dialects, turns GREAT into **gert** and which, in Standard English, has produced the word BIRD from Old English *brid*.

The Old Norse-influenced northern area is seen to be large in this map, suggesting that BRIG is vigorously supported. However, it does appear that BRIDGE, the Standard English word, is encroaching on this area in what Trudgill describes as "a rather interesting way" (*Dialects of England*, 124). As Trudgill points out, BRIDGE appears to have become established around the coastal cities of Sunderland and Grimsby, from where it is spreading inland and along the coast. This is just one example of the effect of growing urban areas and communications on language change in general and on the erosion of traditional dialect in particular.

# BRUSH

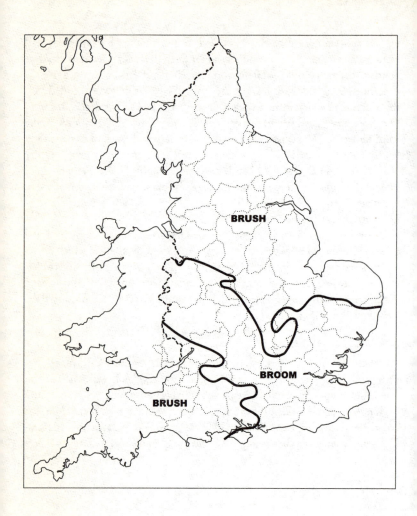

MAP 72
# BRUSH for sweeping

As is frequently the case with the adoption of words, the choice between BRUSH and BROOM as the word for the ordinary long-handled domestic sweeping implement shows the dominance of a newer term over an older one.

In Old English the word for the implement was *brōm*, pronounced **brome**. The word applied to the broom plant, just as it does today, the name incidentally coming from a Germanic base-word which also gives us BRAMBLE. Since twigs, frequently broom twigs, were originally used for sweeping, it was reasonable for the name BROOM to be transferred from the plant to the sweeping implement also. BROOM is found scattered throughout those areas where BRUSH is dominant.

BRUSH is an importation into English from Old French, entering the language probably in the later Middle English period. It is tempting to suppose that, like BROOM, there is a connection between the word for the sweeping implement and vegetation, in this case through the idea of 'brushwood'. However, whilst BRUSH with the 'brushwood' meaning is descended from Old French *broce* and Anglo-Norman *bruce*, in the 'sweeping-brush' sense it derives from Old French *broisse*, so that in English at least there is no connection between the two, although it is quite possible that there is a connection between the two further back in European linguistic history.

It is normal to expect that Middle English and early Modern English innovations, especially innovations which become very widely current, should have their beginnings in the area around London and the university cities of Oxford and Cambridge, the area which has given us the ***synecdochic*** or ***hegemonic*** dialect by which other dialects have come to be judged. This has apparently not been so in the case of BRUSH, as BROOM is firmly established in that area of powerful cultural influence on the language.

# CHIMNEY

MAP 73
# CHIMNEY

Whereas it is clear from their histories that the closely-related BRIDGE and BRIG should be regarded as separate words on Map 71, it is not possible to say with complete certainty whether one is dealing with separate words or with different forms of the same word when considering the items here. All are clearly formed on the standard word CHIMNEY, and most, particularly CHIMLEY and CHIMBLEY, are only slightly different from it: these could be regarded as variant pronunciations rather than as separate items of dialect vocabulary. However, others, most noticeably CHIMMOCK and an unmapped Yorkshire form CHIMBLET, are rather more considerable variants. Clearly, in certain cases more is occurring than simply alteration of pronunciation, and the regional differences should arguably be given equal status by the dialectologist.

Two unusual dialect words for CHIMNEY are not shown on the map. LUM was recorded in Northumberland as meaning both the chimney and the chimney-flue. The *Shorter Oxford English Dictionary* records LUM as being a Scottish and Northern English word, originally meaning an opening or skylight in a roof in the sixteenth century and then, from the seventeenth century, a chimney or chimney-top. It is probably derived from the Old French word *lum*, 'light', and connected with the French word *lumière* in its meaning 'an aperture or passage'.

The other word not mapped is TUN, found in Wiltshire. The dictionary records this, meaning 'chimney' and particularly that part of the chimney projecting above the roof of a house (the chimney-stack), from the late Middle English period, stating that it is now dialectal. It is, as the dictionary indicates, an extension of TUN meaning 'barrel' to the similarly-shaped chimney-top.

# COAL DUST

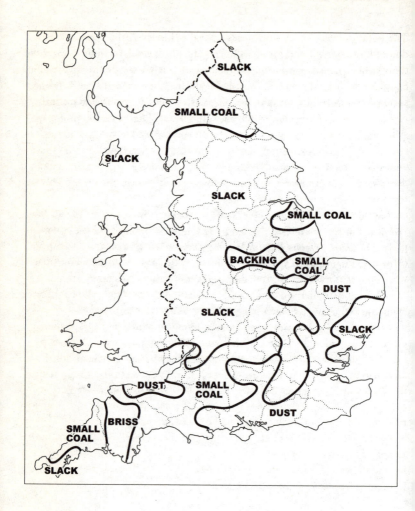

MAP 74
# COAL DUST

The notion of very small, fine pieces of coal which might be used to keep a domestic fire smouldering for a long time is one which yields many synonyms in the non-standard dialects. Furthermore, this variety is to some extent mirrored in Standard English, with no single word being likely to be accepted by all standard speakers as the obvious one to choose. This can be the case with many domestic objects or concepts which are unlikely to be spoken about beyond a fairly restricted neighbourhood, and people who may habitually use widely known, standard words for many aspects of their lives are likely to use the local words when speaking about such things. Even after the normalizing effect of supermarkets and large butchery chains, there remains a great deal of local variation in the names of cuts of meat, with RUMP STEAK for example being called, amongst other local names, FRY STEAK, HIP BONE STEAK, JUNK, PIN BONE, SHELL BONE, STEAK PIECE, and STEAK BONE. Sometimes also the same words are used in different places to denote different things: BROOM is used in places as a name for GORSE (Map 68); many people experience difficulty over the precise meaning of the words CRUMPET, PIKELET, PANCAKE, and MUFFIN.

Recorded in Wright's *Dialect Dictionary* with reference to kindling wood, BRISS may be related to BREEZE, which Wright collected with a precise 'coal-dust' meaning and which the *Shorter Oxford English Dictionary* defines as 'small cinders, coke dust etc., often used with sand and cement to make lightweight building blocks (*breeze-blocks*)'. BRISS can be variously BRISS COAL and BRISSY COAL, adding to the variety of terminology by simple extension of the basic form. Similarly, DUST is COAL DUST, DUST COAL and DUSTY COAL. SLACK may also be SLACK COAL, while the close variant SLATCH has been found in Dorset and the probably related word SLAG in Yorkshire, Oxfordshire, and Surrey.

Words such as DUST and SMALL COAL are of course purely descriptive, and BACKING too is descriptive in denoting coal which is used to 'back' the fire, damping the flames with a layer of very small pieces which will smoulder instead of burning quickly and brightly.

# EASTER EGG

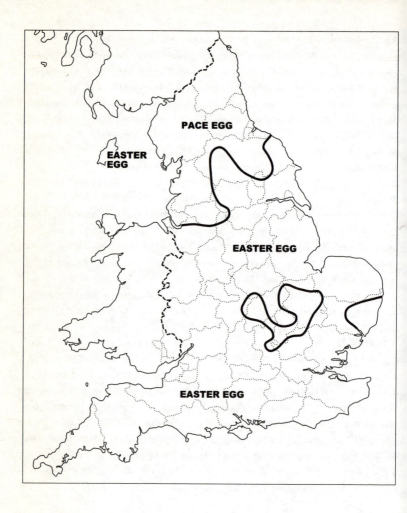

MAP 75
# EASTER EGG

An egg is apparently lifeless, but from it new life emerges. It was originally a pagan symbol of life, but in the Christian religion it has come to be closely associated with Easter, when Christ's resurrection is celebrated. The term EASTER EGG is therefore entirely understandable, but PACE EGG is more obscure. PACE is a northern dialect form of an archaic word *Pasch*, pronounced **pask** or **pahsk**. *Pasch* in turn derives from the Hebrew word for the Jewish festival of Passover, but it has been used since Old English times to refer to Easter, the Christian festival which occurs at approximately the same time. Its best-known Modern English form is probably the little-used adjective *paschal*, with reference being made in Christian liturgy to Jesus as the *paschal lamb*, 'the lamb sacrificed at Passover/Easter'.

Today's chocolate Easter eggs are a development from the hard-boiled eggs which have traditionally been decorated and given as gifts at Easter throughout the country and which, apparently in Northern England especially, have been the subject of a wide variety of customs. Egg-rolling has been a particularly popular custom, as has 'pace-egging', the performing of plays around towns and villages at Easter in return for gifts of eggs or money. In Chester the bishop, dean, and choristers were at one time accustomed to throw eggs in the cathedral during the Easter service!

Although today Easter eggs are well known everywhere, this has apparently not always been so. As the map shows, in some parts of the East Midlands, east Warwickshire, and East Anglia no traditional word for EASTER EGG has been collected. In these areas speakers often said that such eggs were not known until quite recent times. The student of dialect vocabulary must always be aware that the richness of information concerning particular semantic fields may be regionally conditioned with, for example, mining terms or words connected with sheep-farming being well understood and highly detailed in one place but unknown in another nearby.

# APRIL FOOL

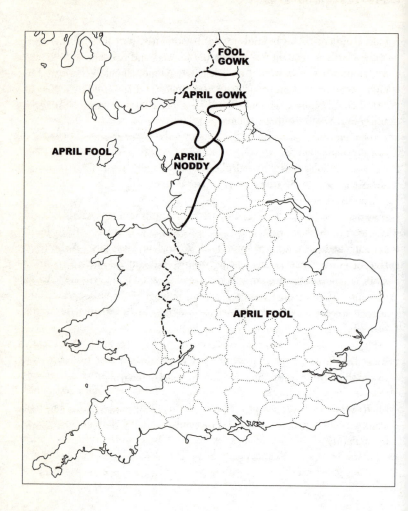

FOOL
GOWK

APRIL GOWK

APRIL FOOL

APRIL
NODDY

APRIL FOOL

MAP 76

# APRIL FOOL

In England 1 April may be known as APRIL FOOL'S DAY, ALL FOOLS' DAY, or in parts of the North as APRIL NODDY DAY. In the Borders and Scotland it is known as HUNTIGOWK DAY or GOWKIN' DAY. Tricks are traditionally played between midnight and noon. Anyone trying to play a trick after midday is told something like: "April Fool's gone past, | You're the biggest fool at last" or "April Noddy's past and gone, | You're the fool and I am none".

The use of APRIL FOOL is quite consistent over most of England, with occasional variations to OLD FOOL or shortening to FOOL. It is therefore remarkable that areas of Northern England should see the use of two very different but well-attested forms, GOWK and NODDY.

The word GOWK is descended from the Old Norse *gaukr*, 'a cuckoo'. It is recorded as having been used to mean 'a fool' in English since the late sixteenth century but can be expected to have had a continuous existence in the North since the Viking period. The preceding of GOWK with APRIL is quite understandable, of course, in order to particularize the foolishness to April the First. FOOL GOWK is a more curious form, which translates as 'fool fool' and is evidence that the unusual word GOWK has lost its precise significance in one area at least.

Like GOWK, NODDY has a long history of referring to a fool or simpleton, first being recorded with that meaning in the early sixteenth century. The name presumably derives from an uncoordinated or sleepy nodding of the head. A variant April Fool form NIDDY-NODDY has been recorded in Lancashire, this being recorded in the *Shorter Oxford English Dictionary* referring to unsteady movements.

Dialect words concerning silliness or stupidity are very numerous in the nonstandard dialects. Some of these are listed and a few discussed in detail at the map for SILLY (Map 47).

MAP 77
# AUTUMN

Although it is not recorded with this meaning before the middle of the sixteenth century, it is reasonable to suppose that the Old English word FALL was applied much earlier to the season when leaves drop from the trees. FALL is the usual word used in North America and is today chiefly associated with that part of the world. Nevertheless, in spite of its modern American associations it is seen to retain a strong presence in England, where it occurs alone as a *simplex* form or is used to create compound expressions such as FALL OF THE LEAF and FALL OF THE LEAVES (chiefly in the east) or FALL OF THE YEAR.

BACKEND is seen to be the dominant non-standard word in Northern England and the North Midlands. Like FALL, BACKEND may occur in compound expressions, in this case as BACKEND OF (THE) YEAR. Sometimes, cold weather which hints at the approach of winter can be heard to be described as BACKENDISH. Indeed, the *Shorter Oxford English Dictionary* specifically states that BACKEND applies to 'the later part of the year, late autumn', although in the non-standard dialects at least this narrow application of the word to a particular part of autumn is not necessarily required.

The modern standard word AUTUMN is an importation into English from French, beginning to be used during the Middle English period. Today it is spreading out from its firm base in South-eastern England, being used widely alongside non-standard words wherever these are found.

A form similar to BACKEND, LATTER END, has been recorded in use in Kent, and the similarly-influenced AFTER-SEASON has been found in Cornwall.

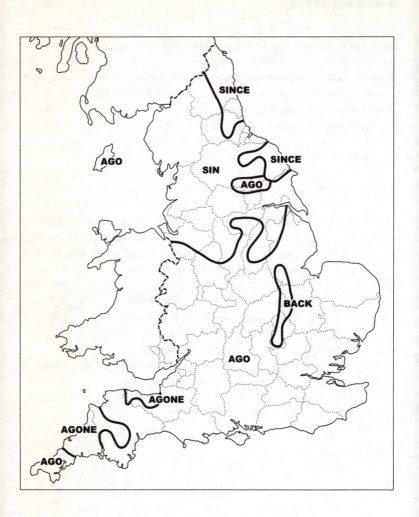

MAP 78

# a week AGO

AGO and its dialect synonyms are ***postpositive*** adjectives, only being placed after the noun which they modify.

Both AGO and AGONE are Middle English and are simply different forms of the same word. The *Shorter Oxford English Dictionary* lists AGONE as archaic, and quotes Shakespeare's *Twelfth Night* "He's drunk, … an hour agone": clearly the word was formerly in more general use than it is now. AGO is used generally in all the English counties except the most northerly.

SIN and SINCE, as one would expect, are also closely related words. However, it is not the case that SIN is simply an abbreviation of SINCE: in fact both SIN and SINCE are derived from a common source. In Old English there was a versatile word of which a rather more modern version is *sithen* and which had such meanings as 'since', 'ago', 'then', and 'afterwards'. SIN is a short version of this old word *sithen*, as too is SINE which, although not mapped, has been recorded meaning AGO in two places in Northumberland and Durham. SINE is very well known in Scotland (where it is usually spelt *syne*) and has become particularly famous around the world from the song *Auld Lang Syne* (literally 'old long ago'), which is often sung at New Year celebrations. In the Middle English period *sithen* acquired a final -*s* by the same process by which AFTERWARD and BESIDE acquired it (see AMONG, Map 27). The extended word was normally spelt *sithence*, and it is this word which ultimately came to be shortened to SINCE.

It is not surprising to find BACK used as a synonym for AGO, given its widespread colloquial use in this sense and its standard dialect use with connotations of 'time past' in such expressions as 'to think back' or 'back in the old days'. PAST has been recorded meaning AGO in Berkshire.

# PLAY

MAP 79
# to PLAY

Although it shows a very simple division between PLAY and LAKE, it is virtually essential that this map should appear in any collection of maps of regional words in England. Along with GINNELL and SNICKET to denote footpaths running between buildings, LAKE (sometimes spelt LAIK) in place of standard PLAY is considered by many to be especially characteristic of Northern English vocabulary although, as can be seen, it is not recorded in the northernmost counties.

As well as characterizing Northern speech, the existence of LAKE exemplifies the fact that when dialect words are being compared it is often impossible to identify those which are completely synonymous. Here LAKE and PLAY, having been collected in response to the Survey of English Dialects 'completing' question "In their holidays some children like to work, but most like to …", both imply the taking of recreational exercise. LAKE, however, has meanings relating to taking time away from work, either officially (as in 'the mills are laking') or without permission. PLAY, being used in both standard and non-standard speech, has in its turn a range of meanings which is more extensive than that of LAKE (for example 'lightheartedly make fun of someone', 'perform on an instrument', 'take part in a game'). The fact that two words coincide in one of their meanings should not be taken to imply that they can be compared at every point. Indeed, it is to be questioned whether there is such a thing as absolute synonymy.

LAKE is apparently an example, with TEEM ('pour'), WHIN ('gorse'), SPELL ('splinter'), LUG ('ear'), NEB ('beak')—Maps 87, 68, 55, 42, and 64 respectively—and very many others, of a word which owes its present location and strong speaker support to its Viking origins. There was in fact an Old English word *lācan*, 'to play', but this was paralleled by the Old Norse *leika* which, to judge from the Viking-settled area in which LAKE is now to be found, is the true ancestor of the modern word. PLAY, in contrast, is a purely English-derived word. Both PLAY and LAKE have in their original meanings basic notions of taking exercise and moving busily about, from which later meanings connected with recreation have developed.

# BOUNCE

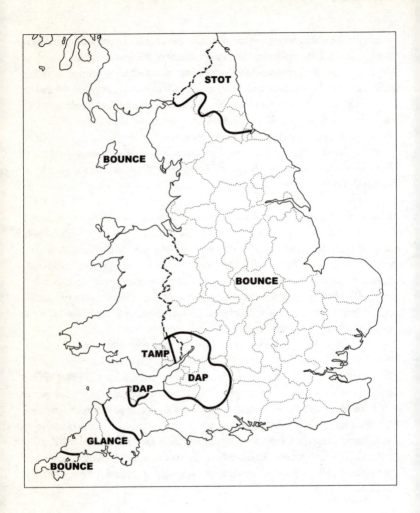

MAP 80

# to BOUNCE, describing a ball

The Standard English word used to describe the action of a rebounding ball, BOUNCE, is very firmly established in the non-standard dialects of England: these of course are strongly influenced by the standard, particularly when some quite common notion needs to be expressed.

However, regional words used to express the idea of bouncing appear to remain strong in a few places. In one case in particular the strength of the localized form is especially reinforced by association with a particular commonplace object. DAP, found not only in the south-west Midlands and the South-west as mapped here but also in much of Wales, is the word used in those areas in place of standard GYMSHOE to describe a rubber-soled sports shoe. This is variously known elsewhere as a PUMP in much of the North and Midlands, a SANDSHOE in the North-east, and a PLIMSOLL in the South-east and South. The *Shorter Oxford English Dictionary* considers that DAP referring to a shoe may be a different word from that referring to a ball: if this is so there is nevertheless surely a link through the bouncing action of a ball and that of the wearer of gymshoes. It would appear that DAP, first recorded meaning 'bounce' in the mid-nineteenth century but earlier having meant 'to fish by making bait bob lightly on the water', is connected with both DAB and the more obscure word DOP. DOP is a development of an Old English word meaning 'to baptize', and this in turn has links with Old English *dyppan*, 'to dip': DAP, DAB, DOP, and DIP are thus all linked, as also, a little more remotely, is DEEP.

The dictionary records STOT meaning 'to bounce' in Scotland and Northern England in the early sixteenth century. There is also a word STOIT, meaning 'to bounce' or 'to lurch', which is chiefly used in Scotland and has possible Old Norse connections.

With their respective connections with rapid or up-and-down movement, it is not surprising to find GLANCE and TAMP applied to a bouncing action. In parts of South Wales someone who is very angry and agitated is said to be 'tamping mad'.

# CHOKE or STRANGLE

MAP 81

# to CHOKE or STRANGLE someone with one's hands

The dominant words on this map, CHOKE and THROTTLE, are both of Old English origin, whereas the other well-known word shown, STRANGLE, is derived from Old French and did not enter English until the Middle English period. It is clear from evidence such as this that the new medieval French imports into the language, whilst often being taken into the standard dialect, may have made little impact on non-standard speech even after many centuries of use.

The verb TO CHOKE is formed from the same Old English word that gives us modern English *cheek*. In the Old English period *cheek* was used to describe the jaw as well as the side of the face, and the original force of the word included ideas of smothering as well as that of constricting the neck which it has today. THROTTLE seems to be a **diminutive** of *throat*, so that its earliest meaning would have been 'little throat'. Although it is normally used as a verb it can also be used as a noun, meaning 'a throat': conversely, THROAT, not mapped here, has been recorded in Norfolk meaning 'to choke'. Other words not mapped include the similar-sounding and perhaps related CRACKLE in Essex and QUACKLE in Norfolk, and STIFLE, also used in Essex. In the absence of any evidence to the contrary it is likely that THROPPLE, which can be used as a verb and as a noun, is a northern version of THROTTLE, though we should be wary of making such assumptions.

The meaning of the verbs used here shows that all are **transitive**: all refer to an action taken against a direct object. Of the words shown, however, only CHOKE can be used as an **intransitive** verb, without a direct object: a person can choke as well as choking someone else, but they cannot throttle, or thropple, or strangle—they can only do this to another person.

Two of the words here have in the present century undergone a very marked **semantic extension**: both CHOKE and THROTTLE have come to be applied to the new technology of the automotive industry, although interestingly in this new context they have acquired separate, if closely-related, meanings. Languages often make use of such extension to cope with the advent of new technologies.

# CLIMB

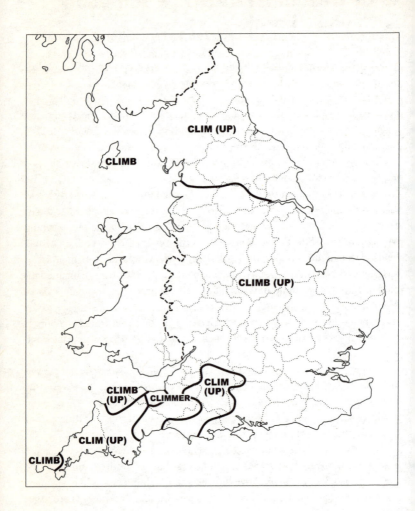

MAP 82

# to CLIMB

This apparently simple map presents a wide variety of linguistic information. The distinction between CLIMB and CLIM, as with that between CURSE and CUSS (Map 83), is one of phonology or lexis, while that between these and CLIMMER is one of lexis only. CLIMB belongs to a group of words which end in a *b* which is not pronounced, a matter of phonology. And CLIMB and CLIM can each be followed by the preposition UP and are examples of a grammatical word-class known loosely as *phrasal*, or more exactly as *prepositional*, *verbs*. (For phrasal verbs created with adverbs, see POUR, Map 87.)

The history of the pronunciation of the vowel in CLIMB in Standard English is that discussed at the map for FIND (Map 9), with an Old English short **i** sound becoming first lengthened and then diphthongized. The survival of the original **i** in Northern England, clearly seen in the FIND map, is seen too in the existence of northern CLIM here; elsewhere in England CLIMB has the kind of variety of pronunciation which is seen to exist for FIND.

That the **i** pronunciation here is not confined to the North as it is for FIND is due to the fact that the CLIMB/CLIM distinction is not *entirely* one of pronunciation. As Joseph and Elizabeth Wright point out (*New English Grammar*, para. 354), from Middle English times until the seventeenth century CLIMB had a wide variety of acceptable forms. One of these was CLIM, written *clim* or *climme* and with a past tense *clam* (*clamme*) or *climmed* and a *past participle clum* or *climmed*. CLIM is therefore not simply a **klim** pronunciation of CLIMB, but has clearly had an independent existence as a word. It is this word which has apparently given rise to the localized CLIMMER in the West Country.

The presence of a written *b* in such words as CLIMB is discussed by Ekwall in *English Sounds and Morphology* (para. 168). Although the **b** was originally pronounced, there is evidence that it had ceased to be so throughout England in the sixteenth century, and that its loss had occurred in the North much earlier, around 1300. As the spelling convention had been established, however, -*b* remained for CLIMB and also for such words as COMB, LAMB, and WOMB. Curiously, some other words which originally ended with -*m* acquired a written -*b* once **b** had ceased to be pronounced, giving us for example LIMB and NUMB from Middle English *lim* and *nume*.

# CURSE

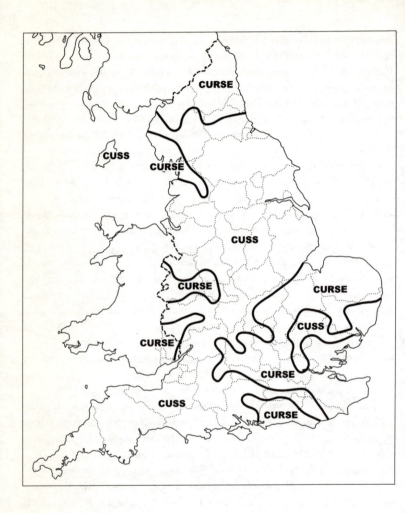

MAP 83

# to CURSE and swear

It is possible to argue that the difference between CURSE and CUSS, like that between CLIMB and CLIM (Map 82), is either one of vocabulary or of pronunciation. Both are obviously pronunciation forms of the same word, of which the standard representation is CURSE. However, it appears that many people make use of both forms. CURSE is very likely to be used by such people as their normal word, but CUSS may be selected for use in certain situations, most particularly when a colloquial style of language is required and very often when used alongside TO SWEAR in such phrases as 'cursing/cussing and swearing'. (This is especially likely to be the case when another non-standard word such as BLINDING is substituted for SWEARING.)

CURSE, both as a noun and a verb, is found in Old English. Pronunciation of the word at that period involved a short vowel sound, short **oo**, with the *r* of the spelling pronounced after it. During the early Modern English period the **oo** sound developed into an **uh**, so that the whole word was typically pronounced **kuhrs**. The development of this **-uhr-** combination in Modern British English has been for **r** to cease to be pronounced (Dobson, *English Pronunciation 1500–1700*, para. 401), and for the short **uh** to be lengthened to **er**. (This last **r** is only given here to suggest the length of the sound: it should not be pronounced, as it would be in American English.) It is therefore not hard to see how the widely used CUSS form and the well-known colloquial adjective CUSSED (**kuhsid**) may have come into existence. The Old or Middle English short sound, **oo** or **uh**, has survived, but the **r** has been dropped just as it has been in the standard form CURSE.

The *Shorter Oxford English Dictionary* regards CUSS as coming originally from the United States of America. It is likely therefore that CUSS has frequently received separate word status in the USA and that the written form of the word emanates from there, with the British form being seen by its users as simply a variant pronunciation of CURSE and therefore seldom being written down. An indication of the divorce of CURSE from CUSS in the minds of some speakers is the fact that the dictionary states that the latter, when applied to a person (someone who is perverse or detestable), has sometimes been taken to be an abbreviation of CUSTOMER.

# DIG

MAP 84
# to DIG

Of the three words shown on this map, DIG, the standard and most widely used, appears to be the newest, being first recorded in Middle English, whilst DELVE and GRAVE are known to have been used in Old English. However, it is likely that DIG is in fact closely related to DITCH, which is to be found in Old English, and that DIG is therefore also from the same period. The literature dating from the Old English period is not very extensive, and the fact that a word is not to be found in what writings exist does not mean that it was not used at that time.

Both DELVE and GRAVE are well-known Modern English words, but in Standard English neither now refers directly to digging with a spade, having undergone *semantic shift*. DELVE now generally means to investigate or research into something, which meaning it took late in the Middle English period, or to reach into something with the hand, this meaning only being acquired in the mid-twentieth century. The noun corresponding to the verb DELVE, DELF, meaning an excavation, has died out completely. GRAVE of course retains its connection with the earth in the standard dialect. However, it is no longer used there as a verb, keeping only the very specific meaning of a place dug to receive a dead body, which is only one of several meanings which the noun once had. The fact that GRAVE is to be found on both sides of Northern England suggests that its use was once far more widespread than it now is: its precise location suggests that it owes its presence in considerable part to the influence of Old Norse, in which it is also found.

Two words not mapped are HOWK (pronounced **hoke**) and SPIT. HOWK, recorded only in two places in Northumberland, was used in Middle English but is now little known: it is distantly related to the modern words HOLLOW and HOLE. SPIT, which is connected with the object on which meat is roasted through the idea of 'a pointed rod or stick' (which could be used for digging), was used as a verb in Old English and is recorded from Somerset. Nowadays it is more commonly used as a noun, in Standard English referring to a spadeful of earth and in Northumberland to a spade.

Especially in the South-west and in Norfolk some speakers prefer to replace a single verb with such phrases as TURN THE GROUND UP or TURN THE EARTH OVER.

# PANT

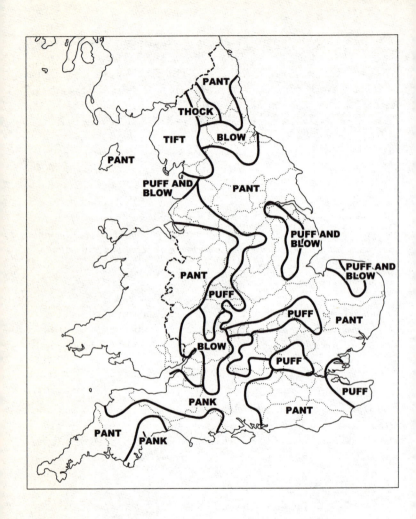

MAP 85

# to PANT

The standard word used to describe breathing hard after running or other vigorous exercise, PANT, is derived from the Old French word *pantaisier*, 'to be agitated, gasp, pant'. Like many other French-derived words, it entered Middle English and supplanted existing terms not only in standard usage but as the normal regionalism in many places too.

Precisely what word or words PANT supplanted on its arrival in English is unclear. PUFF is a possible candidate: it is ***imitative*** of the sound of panting and so has a very simple derivation, suggesting an ancient origin; also the *Shorter Oxford English Dictionary* suggests that there was an Old English verb *pyffan*, although this is not recorded meaning 'to pant' before late Middle English times. Similarly BLOW, from Old English *blāwan*, is found to mean 'to pant' in late Middle English, so it is possible that both PUFF and BLOW, often associated in the phrase TO PUFF AND BLOW for many speakers even beyond those areas showing it on the map, predate PANT in English usage.

Of the remaining words mapped two, PANK and TIFT, can be explained as ***variants*** of standard words, while the other, THOCK, is obscure. PANK is almost certainly simply a form of PANT. That such a variant can arise, and that it may establish itself in one region rather than appearing more widely, may be remarked upon more readily than explained: a non-standard variant can be taken up and retained by a local population as its own in the face of the existence of a powerful standard near-relation. TIFT, recorded by the dictionary as a noun meaning 'a puff or breath of wind' from the mid-eighteenth century, is apparently connected with TIFF in its senses concerning outbursts of temper and quarrelling. Like many other non-standard dialect words, THOCK can be recorded and mapped but its ***etymology*** or word-history cannot readily be explained.

Other words recorded for TO PANT include BELLOWS, BUSSOCK, HEAVE, HUFF, LALL, PUMP, and WAFF. LALL may be connected with a word derived from Latin which means 'to utter meaningless sounds' and which gives us the word LULLABY, with the idea of LOLLING out the tongue, or with both. However, as with THOCK, it is as well not to invent fanciful etymologies for obscure non-standard words.

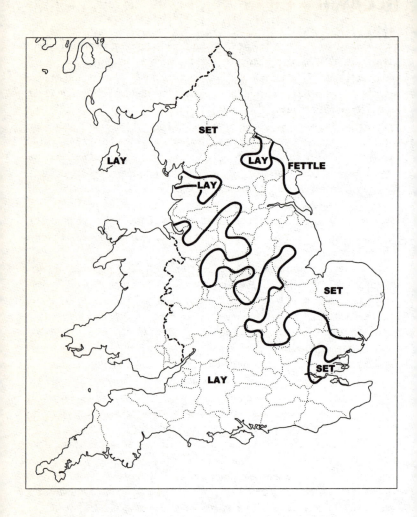

MAP 86
# to LAY the table

There is no obvious reason for the remarkable division of England between the northern and eastern area where SET is preferred and that in the south and west where the preference is for the more standard word LAY. Both words are to be found in Old English and are recorded with the meaning relevant here in Middle English, and both have related or cognate forms in Old Norse. The English/Norse distinction which is often to be seen to have caused regional preferences in word-use does not seem to apply here, and the fact that LAY is the standard word has not resulted in its universal adoption in south-eastern England.

The object of the verb TO LAY can be either the table itself, the tablecloth, or the meal which is placed on it, resulting in such expressions as LAY (THE) TABLE, LAY THE BOARD, LAY THE (TABLE-)CLOTH, and LAY THE DINNER. The object of TO SET is restricted to the table or the meal, giving for example SET (THE) TABLE and SET THE TEA with variations such as SET THE TABLE OUT, SET THE TEA OUT. FETTLE is restricted in its object to the meal, giving FETTLE THE TEA. Now a little-known word, FETTLE, like LAY and SET, has an Old English origin and a relevant Middle English meaning, 'to make ready, arrange'.

Used in its standard sense here to mean 'arrange or spread out in position', LAY is frequently used by non-standard speakers in place of LIE, giving rise to such expressions as 'go and lay down'. The two verbs have separate English histories, LAY being *lecgan* in Old English and LIE being *licgan*, although both stem originally from the same Germanic root. Non-standard use of LAY for standard LIE is no doubt partly the result of the fact that LAY is the past-tense form of LIE as well as being a verb in its own right. That some speakers use LIE to replace the more standard LAY to produce such expressions as LIE THE TABLE reinforces the impression that the LAY/LIE distinction has always been rather blurred by English speakers.

# POUR

POUR

POUR

POUR

TEEM

POUR

MAP 87

# to POUR tea

Both POUR and TEEM are first recorded in use in Middle English. POUR is of obscure origin, whilst TEEM is descended from Old Norse *tœma* 'to empty'. It seems likely that both words existed in some form in the Old English period, perhaps with POUR dominant over much of England as it is today and TEEM used in the North in the areas of main Viking settlement. POUR is by far the more dominant word, being recorded virtually throughout the country in non-standard as well as in standard use and apparently now having crossed the Humber to spread up the East Yorkshire coast. However, TEEM continues to maintain a strong presence, and it is even stronger and more widespread when used to describe the action of steady, heavy rain.

Other less widespread synonyms of POUR are BIRLE in Cumberland, EMPT in Somerset, and the associated ENT in Cornwall, HALE or HELL in Dorset, LADE and LADEN in Cheshire, and SHOOT in Somerset. POUR and other such words often function as phrasal verbs followed by the adverb OUT: compare CLIMB (Map 82), for prepositional verbs; verbs comprising verb + preposition are not usually regarded by grammarians as true phrasal verbs like those comprising verb + adverb, but the two may be loosely grouped together.

Although there are several dialect synonyms of POUR, the dialect situation is straightforward because most words are found in use in small areas. This is less so for words describing the related processes of pouring boiling water onto tea-leaves and waiting for the resultant liquid to strengthen: unfortunately the question asked of informants in the Survey of English Dialects for this notion makes it impossible positively to distinguish between the 'making' and 'infusing' processes. A wide range of terms is recorded, including SOAK and WET in the South-west, MASH in the North and Midlands, and MASK in the extreme North. One standard word for making tea is of course BREW, borrowed, like MASH, MASK, and perhaps other terms, from ale- and beer-brewing when the need arose for new terminology at the introduction of tea into England.

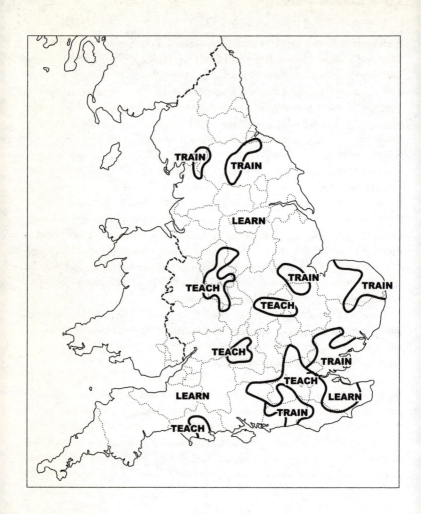

MAP 88

# to TEACH a dog

There is clear demarcation between TEACH and LEARN in Standard English, with TO TEACH meaning to pass knowledge to someone and TO LEARN meaning to receive it. Historically, however, and in the non-standard dialects, there is considerable overlap between the two words, an overlap which is noticeably paralleled in the third word mapped, TO TRAIN, which can mean both to instruct ('He trains footballers') and to receive instruction ('She is training to be a doctor').

TEACH is originally an Old English word, with early meanings ranging from those concerned with the general sharing of information to those corresponding to that of modern Standard English. In its earliest English form it is related to modern TOKEN.

LEARN existed in Old English as *leornian*, and unsurprisingly its earliest meaning is 'to acquire knowledge'; a somewhat similar Old English word, *lǣran*, meant 'to teach'. During the Middle English period the two words tended to fall together as *lerne*, which meant both 'to learn' and 'to teach', and the latter usage, now markedly non-standard, can be seen to be favoured by the majority of non-standard dialect speakers providing information for this map. The *Shorter Oxford English Dictionary* glosses this use of the word as 'non-standard', implying that it is not geographically restricted, and this is seen to be broadly true. Its use is so all-pervading that TEACH and TRAIN have been able to sustain regional popularity only over relatively small and isolated regions.

Another pair of words like TEACH and LEARN which displays noticeable overlap in standard and non-standard use is BORROW and LEND. It would be interesting to investigate whether these words have distinct regional distributions.

The third word mapped, TRAIN, is of French origin, and in its first use in Middle English concerned dragging and hauling. It was not until the end of the Middle English period that it acquired meanings concerned with direction and control, and it was the sixteenth century before it came to mean 'to educate'. Its use meaning 'to undergo a course of instruction' developed in the seventeenth century.

# THROW

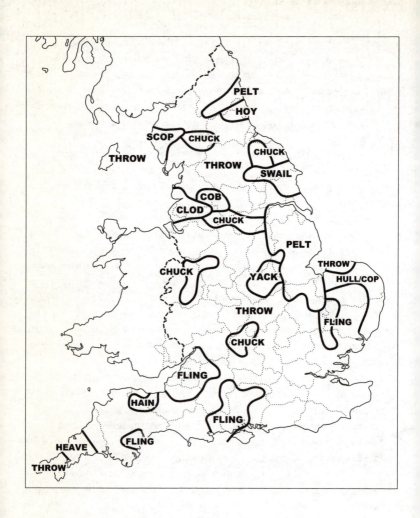

MAP 89

# to THROW

The standard word THROW is to be found in use by non-standard speakers throughout England, in all areas where other words are seen to be used. THROW itself is Old English in origin, but its usual Old English meaning was 'to twist, to turn', and it was not until the Middle English period that it came to be associated predominantly with such senses as 'to propel something through the air'. Although words are sometimes very old we are constantly confronted by change of meaning, or semantic shift: *word* and *meaning* are not identical concepts.

Most of the other words mapped are, in their connection with throwing, purely non-standard dialect. Those which have some wider currency in the language are CHUCK, CLOD, HEAVE, and PELT, all of which can be dated to the late Middle to early Modern English period. CHUCK is first recorded in the early sixteenth century meaning 'to knock, to bump': its earliest connection with throwing dates from the late seventeenth century in a reference to a coin-throwing game, *chuck-farthing*. CLOD is found in the early sixteenth century, understandably meaning 'to pelt with clods of earth or with stones'. HEAVE, with its connotations of hard physical effort, comes to mean 'to throw something heavy' in the late sixteenth century. And PELT, connected through Latin with the Basque ball-game of *pelota*, is first recorded in English in the late fifteenth century.

It is in the variety of words used to render a very simple everyday concept that the main interest of this notion lies, however, and in *Dialects of England* (114) Trudgill uses the list of words mapped here, words "uncovered by *The Survey of English Dialects*", as telling evidence that "the richness of Traditional Dialect vocabulary is very considerable". As greater evidence of the truth of this assertion we can go on to list the other words for THROW uncovered by the Survey, but not mapped since they do not cluster in significantly large geographical areas: AIM, CHECK, CLOT, COBBLE, HANG, HOCKS, HOLL, HOY, JERK, PEG, PITCH, SHOOT, SHY, SLEW, SLING, SOCK, STONE, TOSS, WHANG, and YARK. An initial list of fourteen words thus expands to thirty-four.

MAP 90

# STOP!, a call to horses

WO is sometimes written *woa* and perhaps today most usually *whoa*. Although it is possible that the different written, or **orthographic**, forms used occasionally imply differences in pronunciation—perhaps **wo-uh** for the spelling with final *a*, or **hwo** or **hwo-uh** for that containing *h*—the findings of the Survey of English Dialects suggest that this is not regularly so, and that the spellings are usually merely the preferences of different writers. That being so, WO is the form chosen to be used here, since not only is its written form unambiguous, but the *Shorter Oxford English Dictionary* records it in use in the late eighteenth century, WOA and WHOA being later versions dating from the mid-nineteenth century. The dictionary states that the word is found in Middle English with the spelling *who*: this form is avoided here both on the grounds that there is no evidence of **h** in modern pronunciations of the word, and also of course because of the danger of it being confused with the pronoun WHO. Like WOA and WHOA, WAY is recorded as a 'stop!' call for horses from the mid-nineteenth century. It is clearly a variant of WO(WOA/WHOA), so it is remarkable that the different forms have such clear-cut regional distributions, as is the existence of a small area for the remaining variant, WEE.

All the forms shown may have developed from HO, which was found meaning 'halt' in Old French and which seems to have survived as a twentieth-century 'stop!' call to horses in a small area of Cornwall. If this is indeed the origin, the *h* in the *who* and *whoa* spellings is probably indicative of earlier pronunciations in which the **h** was regularly to be heard.

Confusingly, WO has also been used to order 'turn right!' and 'turn left!' in several areas of the country, and HO to order a horse to 'turn right!' in Shropshire. Clearly different horsemen had, and still have, their own preferences, which are only partially influenced by the region in which they work.

Other 'stop!' calls recorded but not mapped are GEE BACK, HALT, HISS, HOLD TIGHT, WAY WO, WOAG, WOAT, WO BACK, WO HO, WO THERE, WUP, and YEA.

# BIBLIOGRAPHY

*Short titles used in the text are shown in square brackets following relevant entries.*

BAUGH, ALBERT C., and CABLE, THOMAS, *A History of the English Language* (4th edn.; London: Routledge, 1993).

BENNETT, J. A. W., and SMITHERS, G. V. (eds.), *Early Middle English Verse and Prose* (2nd edn.; Oxford: Oxford University Press, 1968).

BROOK, G. L., *English Accents* (London: André Deutsch, 1963).

CHAMBERS, J. K., and TRUDGILL, PETER, *Dialectology* (Cambridge: Cambridge University Press, 1980).

DOBSON, E. J., *English Pronunciation 1500–1700* (2nd edn.; Oxford: Oxford University Press, 1968).

EKWALL, EILERT, *A History of Modern English Sounds and Morphology*, trans. and ed. Alan Ward (Oxford: Blackwell, 1975) [*English Sounds and Morphology*].

*English Dialect Dictionary*: see Wright, Joseph

FRANCIS, W. N., *Dialectology: An Introduction* (London: Longman, 1983).

HUGHES, ARTHUR, and TRUDGILL, PETER, *English Accents and Dialects: An Introduction to Social and Regional Varieties of British English* (2nd edn.; London: Edward Arnold, 1979).

JONES, DANIEL, *An Outline of English Phonetics* (9th edn.; Cambridge: W. Heffer and Sons, 1960).

KIRK, JOHN M., SANDERSON, STEWART, and WIDDOWSON, J. D. A., *Studies in Linguistic Geography* (London: Croom Helm, 1985).

KOLB, EDUARD, GLAUSER, BEAT, ELMER, WILLY, and STAMM, RENATE, *Atlas of English Sounds* (Bern: Francke Verlag, 1979).

LEECH, GEOFFREY, DEUCHAR, MARGARET, and HOOGENRAAD, ROBERT, *English Grammar for Today: A New Introduction* (Basingstoke: Macmillan Education, 1982).

NORTH, DAVID J., and SHARPE, ADAM, *A Word Geography of Cornwall* (Redruth: Institute of Cornish Studies, 1980).

ORTON, HAROLD, *Survey of English Dialects (A): Introduction* (Leeds: E. J. Arnold, 1962) [SED].

——, HALLIDAY, WILFRID J., BARRY, MICHAEL V., TILLING, PHILIP M., and WAKELIN, MARTYN F. (eds.), *Survey of English Dialects (B): The Basic Material* (4 vols., each of 3 parts; Leeds: E. J. Arnold, 1962–71).

# BIBLIOGRAPHY

Orton, Harold, and Wright, Nathalia, *A Word Geography of England* (London: Seminar Press, 1974).

——, Sanderson, Stewart, and Widdowson, John, *The Linguistic Atlas of England* (London: Croom Helm, 1978).

*Oxford Dictionary of English Proverbs*, ed. Wilson, F. P. (3rd edn.; Oxford: Oxford University Press, 1970) [*English Proverbs*].

*Oxford English Dictionary,* ed. Simpson, J. A., and Weiner, E. S. C. (2nd edn.; Oxford: Oxford University Press, 1989).

Petyt, K. M., *The Study of Dialect: An Introduction to Dialectology* (London: André Deutsch, 1980).

Quirk, Randolph, Greenbaum, Sidney, Leech, Geoffrey, and Svartvik, Jan, *A Grammar of Contemporary English* (London: Longman, 1972).

*Shorter Oxford English Dictionary*, ed. Brown, Lesley (Oxford: Oxford University Press, 1993).

Skeat, Walter W., *English Dialects* (Cambridge: Cambridge University Press, 1912).

Strang, Barbara, *A History of English* (London: Methuen, 1970).

Trudgill, Peter, *On Dialect: Social and Geographical Perspectives* (Oxford: Blackwell, 1983).

—— *Dialects in Contact* (Oxford: Blackwell, 1986).

—— *The Dialects of England* (Oxford: Blackwell, 1990).

—— and Chambers, J. K. (eds.), *Dialects of English: Studies in Grammatical Variation* (London: Longman, 1991).

Upton, Clive, Sanderson, Stewart, and Widdowson, John, *Word Maps: A Dialect Atlas of England* (London: Croom Helm, 1987).

——, Parry, David, and Widdowson, J. D. A., *Survey of English Dialects: The Dictionary and Grammar* (London: Routledge, 1994).

Wakelin, Martyn F. (ed.), *Patterns in the Folk Speech of the British Isles* (London: Athlone Press, 1972).

—— *English Dialects: An Introduction* (rev. edn.; London: Athlone Press, 1977).

—— *Discovering English Dialects* (4th edn.; Princes Risborough: Shire Publications, 1994).

Wells, J. C., *Accents of English* (3 vols.; Cambridge: Cambridge University Press, 1982).

—— *Longman Pronunciation Dictionary* (Harlow: Longman, 1990).

Wright, Joseph (ed.), *The English Dialect Dictionary* (6 vols.; Oxford: Oxford University Press, 1898–1905).

—— *The English Dialect Grammar* (Oxford: Oxford University Press, 1905) [*Dialect Grammar*].

—— and Wright, Elizabeth Mary, *An Elementary Historical New English Grammar* (Oxford: Oxford University Press, 1924) [*New English Grammar*].

—— —— *An Elementary Middle English Grammar* (2nd edn.; Oxford: Oxford University Press, 1928) [*Middle English Grammar*].

# INDEX OF MAPS

*Reference is to map numbers; underlined letters are the subject of pronunciation maps.*

ACHE 56
ACTIVE (child) 45
ADDER 59
AFRAID 46
AGO (a week ...) 78
AMONG 27
AMONG(ST) 6
APRIL FOOL 76
ARM 15
ARMPIT 41
AUNT(IE) 4
AUTUMN 77

BACKWARDS 28
BEAK 64
BLISTER 54
BOUNCE 80
BOW-LEGGED 49
BRIDGE 71
BRUSH 72
BURIED 1

CABBAGE 22
CAUGHT (cat ... a mouse) 30
CHILD 37
CHIMNEY 73
CHOKE/STRANGLE (someone, with hands) 81
CLIMB 82
COAL DUST 74
CROSS 5
CROSS-EYED 51
CURSE 83
CUSHION 16

DEW 25

DIG 84

EAR (head) 42
EASTER EGG 75

FEMALE CAT 60
FESTER 57
FIND 9
FINGER 20
FIVE 10
FLEA 61
FLITCH 66
FOREHEAD 43
FORWARDS 29

GIDDY 52
GIVE IT ME 26
GOOSEBERRY 67
GORSE 68
GRANDAD 38
GYPSY 40

HAND 2
HEDGEHOG 62
HERS 35
HOUSE 23
HUNGRY 53

INFECTIOUS 58

KNOCK-KNEED 50

LAST 3
LAY (to ... the table) 86

MEAT 12
MOLARS 44

ONLY (... a child) 48

PANT (to ...) 85
PEOPLE 36
PIGEONS (tame) 63
PLAY (to ...) 79
POD (peas) 69
POND 70
POUR (tea) 87
PUPPY 65
PUT 8

QUICK (of fingernail) 19

ROOM 13

SHE 34
SHEEP 11
SILLY (person) 47
SPLINTER (thin piece of wood) 55
STOP! (to horses) 90
STRANGLE/CHOKE (someone, with hands) 81
SUN 7

TEACH (to ... a dog) 88
THREE 21
THROW (to ...) 89
TONGUE 17
TUESDAY 24

WE ARE (oh yes ...!) 32
WE TWO (just ...) 31
WOOL 18
WORKMATE 39

YELLOW 14
YOU (... are) 33

186

# INDEX OF LINGUISTIC TERMS

| Linguistic term | Map where defined or first mentioned |
|---|---|
| adverb | 65, PUPPY |
| adverbially | 28, BACKWARDS |
| alliteration | 54, BLISTER |
| Anglo-Norman | 4, AUNT(IE) |
| aphetic (reduction) | 40, GIPSY |
| attributive (possessive pronoun) | 35, HERS |
| back-formation | 65, PUPPY |
| breaking | 9, FIND |
| closer (phonetic closeness) | 11, SHEEP |
| cognates | 55, SPLINTER |
| collective plural | 63, PIGEONS |
| colloquialism | 42, EAR |
| compound | 41, ARMPIT |
| conjunction | 65, PUPPY |
| conjunctive (possessive pronoun) | 35, HERS |
| contradictory positive | 32, WE ARE |
| descriptive (grammar) | 31, WE TWO |
| determiners | 35, HERS |
| diminutive | 81, CHOKE / STRANGLE |
| diminutive suffix | 65, PUPPY |
| diphthong | 9, FIND |
| direct object | 26, GIVE IT ME |
| disjunctive (possessive pronoun) | 35, HERS |
| double plural | 37, CHILD |
| emphatic | 32, WE ARE |
| ending | 47, SILLY |
| etymology | 85, PANT |
| euphony | 27, AMONG |
| figurative | 53, HUNGRY |
| finally (position in a word) | 17, TONGUE |
| folk etymology | 44, MOLARS |
| fracture | 9, FIND |
| fricative consonants | 20, FINGER |
| fricative *r* | 15, ARM |
| fudged sound | 7, SUN |
| grammar | 26, GIVE IT ME |
| Great Vowel Shift | 43, FOREHEAD |
| *h*-deletion | 23, HOUSE |
| hegemonic | 72, BRUSH |
| hypercorrection | 8, PUT |
| imitative | 85, PANT |
| impersonal pronoun | 33, YOU |
| indefinite article | 4, AUNT(IE) |
| indicators | 23, HOUSE |
| indirect object | 26, GIVE IT ME |
| infinitive | 32, WE ARE |
| International Phonetic Alphabet (IPA) | 2, HAND |
| intransitive | 81, CHOKE / STRANGLE |
| irregular verb | 30, CAUGHT |
| isoglosses | xviii, *Introduction* |
| labial | 8, PUT |
| lexis | 43, FOREHEAD |
| loanword | 30, CAUGHT |
| markers | 23, HOUSE |
| medially (position in a word) | 17, TONGUE |
| metanalysis | 59, ADDER |
| metathesis | 71, BRIDGE |
| Middle English (ME) | 1, BURIED |
| misanalysis | 3, LAST |
| monophthong | 9, FIND |
| monosyllables | 11, SHEEP |
| morphology | 26, GIVE IT ME |

# INDEX OF LINGUISTIC TERMS

| Linguistic term | Map where defined or first mentioned | Linguistic term | Map where defined or first mentioned |
|---|---|---|---|
| nasal consonant | 7, SUN | regularization | 30, CAUGHT |
| neutral | 31, WE TWO | retroflex *r* | 15, ARM |
| nonce-word | 41, ARMPIT | rhoticity | 15, ARM |
| | | Romany | 39, WORKMATE |
| object | 34, SHE | | |
| Old English (OE) | 1, BURIED | schwa | 16, CUSHION |
| Old French | 15, ARM | semantic | 37, CHILD |
| Old Norse (ON) | 5, CROSS | semantic extension | 81, CHOKE / STRANGLE |
| orthographic | 90, STOP | | |
| | | semantic fields | 39, WORKMATE |
| palatal sounds | 16, CUSHION | semantic shift | 84, DIG |
| past participle | 82, CLIMB | semivowels | 18, WOOL |
| personal pronoun, first person plural | | simplex | 77, AUTUMN |
| subject | 32, WE ARE | spatial | 37, CHILD |
| personal pronoun, second person | 33, YOU | spelling pronunciation | 14, YELLOW |
| | | Standard English | 1, BURIED |
| personal pronoun, third person singular feminine | 34, SHE | stem (of verb) | 30, CAUGHT |
| | | strong verb | 30, CAUGHT |
| phonology | 43, FOREHEAD | style | 23, HOUSE |
| phrasal verbs | 82, CLIMB | subject | 34, SHE |
| possessive pronoun | 4, AUNT(IE) | subject complement | 31, WE TWO |
| postpositive (adjectives) | 78, AGO | suffix | 17, TONGUE |
| | | synecdochic | 72, BRUSH |
| predicative (possessive pronoun) | 35, HERS | synonyms | 54, BLISTER |
| | | syntax | 26, GIVE IT ME |
| preposition | 26, GIVE IT ME | | |
| prepositional verbs | 82, CLIMB | TH fronting | 21, THREE |
| prescriptive (grammar) | 31, WE TWO | transitive | 81, CHOKE / STRANGLE |
| present tense, first person plural | 32, WE ARE | tu-vous system, T-V system | 33, YOU |
| pronoun exchange | 32, WE ARE | unaccented syllables | 16, CUSHION |
| prop subject | 31, WE TWO | unmarked | 31, WE TWO |
| | | uvular *r* | 15, ARM |
| r-colouring | 15, ARM | | |
| Received Pronunciation (RP) | 2, HAND | variants | 85, PANT |
| | | voiced, voiceless, voicing | 20, FINGER |
| reduced vowels | 16, CUSHION | weak verb | 30, CAUGHT |
| regular verb | 30, CAUGHT | weakened vowels | 16, CUSHION |

# GENERAL INDEX

*Reference is to map numbers.*

a 4, 35
aback 28
ache 56, 61
active 19, 45
adder 4, 59
addled 47
afeared 46
afraid 46
afraint 46
aft 28
after-season 77
afterward 78
against 27
ago 78
agone 78
ahungered 53
aim 89
All Fools' Day 76
am 32
amidst 27
among, ~st 6, 27
an 4
April, ~ fool, ~ Fool's
  Day, ~ Noddy Day
  76
apron 59
arm 3, 15; ~flop,
  ~hole, ~pit 41
arse-afore 28
arse-first 28
Arthur 21
asparagus 67
auger 59
aunt, ~ie 3, 4; ~y 4
autumn 36, 77
Avon 62
axleteeth 44

baba 38
back 78
back-endish 77

backard 28
backend, ~ of the
  year, ~ of year 77
backing 74; ~-arse
  28
backsyfore 28
backteeth 44
backward, ~s 27, 28,
  29
bairn 37
band 2
bandy, ~-kneed, ~-
  legged 49
barmy 47
basin 16
bass (fish) 15
batchy 47
bath 21
batty 47
be 11, 32
beak 61, 64
beal 57
beautiful 24
beef 66
beg, beggar 65
bellows 85
beside 27, 78; ~s 27
besmirch 58
bess-cat 60
Betty 60
bill 64
bin (= are) 32
birle 87
Birmingham 17
bladder, ~wrack 54
blaster 54
bleat 12
bleb 54
blinding 83
blish 54
blister 54, 55

blob 54
blow 85
blush 1, 54
boatswain 28
bob 67
bog-hole 70
bogey 46
boisterous 45
bond 2
book 13
borrow 14, 88
boss-eyed 51
bosun 28
bothersome 45
bounce 80
bow-footed, ~-legged
  49
bowdy-legged 49
bower-legged 49
box 5
bramble 72
brave 45
breast 66
breeches 11
breeze 74
brew 87
bridge 1, 71
brig 71
briss, ~coal, ~y coal
  74
broad-arrowed 49
brock 62
broom 13, 68, 72, 74
broth 5
brow 43
brush 72
buddy 39
bull 8
bullet 8
bullion 8
bullock 8, 66

burglar, burgle 65
buried, bury 1
bus 6, 7
bush 8
bushel 8
bussock 85
butcher 8
butler, buttle 65
butty 39

cabbage 22
cakey 47
canker 57
captious 58
catch 30, 58; ~ed
  26, 30; ~ing, ~y 58
caught 26, 30
chaff 3, 4
chant 4
cheap 22
check 89
chewers 44
chiel 37
child, ~er, ~ren 37
chimblet 73
chimbley 73
chimley 73
chimmock 73
chimney 73
chine 66
chock, ~-teeth 44
choke 81
chop-teeth 44
chuck 89
chump 42
church 1, 71
clabby 54
clam-pen 53
clammed 53
clamming-hole 53
clamming-house 53

clammy 54
clamp 53
clean 12
cleaty 54
cleeky-feet 49
clibby 54
clidgy 54
clim 82
climb 82
climmer 82
clingy 54
clit, ~tied, ~ty 54
clod 89
close 54
clot 89
cloth 5, 6
clutchy 54
coal dust 74
cobble 89
cock-eyed 51
coffin 16
columbine 16
comb 82
computerize 30
conk 42
contagious 58
cosh 69
cost 5
cousin 16
cowshot 63
cowsort 63
crab-ankled 50
cracked 47
crackers 47
crackle 81
cranky 47
creature 24
cronk 42
cross 5, 6; ~-eyed
    51
crumpet 74
crup 64
curse 82, 83
cushat 63
cushion 16
cushy 63
cuss 82, 83; ~ed 83
customer 83

da 38

dab 80
dace 15
dad 38; ~dy 65
daffy 47
daft 47
dag 57
dam (= pond) 70
dance 4
dap 80
dappy 47
dateless 47
daunt 4
dead 45
deep 80
deer 36
delf 84
delve 84
dew 25; ~-dasher
    49; ~-pond 70;
    ~-sweeper 49
dialect 16
dibby 47
dickoy 40
didakai 40
diddicoy 40
diddik 40
diddikite 40
diddy 40
didkoy 40
dig 84
dike 70
dinglow 40
dingy 47
dinloe, dinlow 40
dip 70, 80
discipline 16
ditch 84
dizzy, ~-headed 52
doak 47
dog 5; ~gy 65
dop 80
dormant 47
Dorset 15
dotty 47
double-knappers 44
doubleteeth 44
dough-bake 47
dub 70
duberous 46
dubious 24

duchess 22
duck-nebbed 64
dulbert 47
dum-hole 70
dummel 47
dust, ~ coal, ~y coal
    74

ear 42
Easter egg 75
Egyptian 40
empt 87
en 26
ent 87
enthuse, enthusiasm
    65
ether (=adder) 59
eyeteeth 44

fall, ~ of the leaf, ~ of
    the leaves, ~ of the
    year 77
famine 16
fammelled 53
farmer 20
father 20
feline 16
female cat 60
feminine 16
fester 57
fettle, ~ the tea 86
fidget, ~s 45
field 11
find 7, 9, 10, 82
finger 9, 20, 21
five 10
flapper 42
flay, ~-boggle,
    ~-crow, ~ed 46
flayth 61
flea 61; ~s 26
fleck (= flea) 61
fleff 61
fleyed 46
flick 66
flish 54
flitch 66
flower 15

fly 46
folk, ~s 36
follow 14
fond 47
fool, ~ gowk 76
foot 6
for 26
forehead 43
forrard, ~s 29
forred 43
forth 29
fortune 24
forward 27, 29; ~s
    27, 28, 29
fought 21
freckened 46
free 21
friend 39
fright, ~ened 46
frim 45
frit, ~ted, ~ten 46
frontwards 29
fry steak 74
fuddled 52
full 8; ~ of vim 45
furbush 68
furra-bush 68
furze 68; ~pig 62
fuzzpig 62
fyoff 61

gall 54
gallied, ~ow, ~y 46
gamp 38
ganging-folk 40
ganning on 45
ganny 38
gant 53
gather 57
gaum, ~less 47
gee back 90
giddy, ~-headed 52
ginnell 79
gipsy 40
give, ~ it me, ~ it to
    me, ~ me it 26
glance 80
glee-eyed 51
gliff, ~ed 46
gloss 5

gob 67
God 52
gog-eyed 51
goggle-eyed 51
gooky 47
gooseberry 67
goosebob 67
goosegob 67
goosegog 67
gorm, ~less 47
gorse 68, 74
gospel 5
gowk 76
Gowkin' Day 76
gramfer 38
gramfy 38
grammer 38
grammy 38
gramp, ~s, ~y 38
gran 38
granda 38
grandad 38
grandada 38
grandfather 38
grandmum 38
grandpa 38
grandpapa 38
grandpop 38
grandsire 38
granfer 38
granfy 38
granma 38
granmam 38
granny 38
gransher 38
grass 4
grave 84
great 71
green 11
Greenwich 11, 22, 28
grinders 44
grit 11
groom 13
grozer, ~-berry 67
gymshoe 80
gyp, ~po, ~pot, ~py
40
gypsy 40

hagworm 59
hale 87

hallow 14
halt 90
hand 2
hang 89
harkener 42
harker 42
Harwich 22
haunch 4
he 11, 32
head 66; ~-light 52
heart 66
heave 85, 89
hedge, ~hog, ~pig
62
hedgy-boar 62
heelway 28
hell 87
her 32, 34, 35; ~n, ~s
35
him 32
hip bone steak 74
his, ~n 35
hiss 90
ho 90
hocks 89
hog 62
hold tight 90
hole 70, 84
holl 69, 89
hollan 70
hollow 84; ~-teeth
44
hoo (= she) 34
hood 13
horse 15
hospital 5
house 23, 43; ~wife
28
howk 84
hoy 89
huck 69
hud 42, 69
huff 85
hull 69
hunger 7; ~ed 53
hungry 53
hunter 7
Huntigowk Day 76
hurked up 50
husk 69
hussif 28

India 25
infecting 58
infectious 58
infective 58
is 32
Isabel 60
it 26, 32

jack, ~teeth 44
jawteeth 44
jay-legged 50
Jenny 60
jerk 89
jimmy 42
jumper (=flea) 61
junk 74

kay-legged 50
keb-footed 49
kid 37
kimit 47
kirk 71
kiss 1
knack-kneed 50
knacky-kneed 50
knap-kneed 50
knappy-kneed 50
knee-knapped 50
knell 1
knock-kneed 49, 50
knocker-kneed 50
knuckle-kneed 50

lade, ~n 87
laik 79
lake (= play) 79
lall 85
lamb 82
land 2
last 4, 7
latching 58
lather 21
Latin 16
latter end 77
lava 21
lay, ~ table, ~ the
board, ~ the cloth,
~ the dinner, ~ the
table, ~ the table-
cloth 86
leaf 12

learn 88
leer, ~y 53
lend 88
liaise, liaison 65
lie, ~ the table 86
light 46
limb 82
link-eyed 51
lish 45
listen 1; ~er 42
lit 46
litty 45
liver 66
lodge 70
loft 5
loin 66
lolling 85
loony 47
loopy 47
lop, ~perd 61
lubber 45
lug 42, 79
lullaby 85
lum 73

Maggie 60
marra 39
marrer 39
marrow 39
mash 87
mask 87
mate 39
matter 57
maulers 44, 67
maze 52; ~d 47
mazy 52
me 11, 26
meadow 14
meat 12, 39
mere (= pond) 70
mermaid 70
merry 1
midgen 61
midget 61
mine 4, 35
moat 70
Moggy 60
molars 44, 67
mole-teeth 44
mong 27
monger 6

mongrel 6
moot 70
moss 5
moth 5
mother 6, 7
mouse 43
much 1
muffin 74
mummers 44
mushers 44
music 24
mutton 66
my 4, 35

nanna 38
nanny 38
nap- 50
napper 42
nature 24
naught but 48
naughty 48
naunt 4
neb 64, 79
niddy-noddy 76
no 48
nobbut 48
noddle 42
noddy 47, 76
noggen 47
Norwich 22
nostril 53
nought but 48
noughty 48
numb 82
nutty 47

odious 25
off 5, 6
offal 66
often 5
old fool 76
on the fidget 45
on the fidgets 45
on the rouk 45
on the wander 45
one 8, 33, 48
only 48
oo (= she) 34
our, ~n, ~s 35
ox liver 66
oxter 41

Pace, ~ egg 75
pal 39
pancake 74
pank 85
pant 85
pap, ~py 38
past 78
pasty-footed 49
path 3, 4
pecker 42, 64
peg 89
pelt 89
people 36
pert 45
phonetic 16
pick 64
pig, ~'s head 66
pigeon 16, 63; ~-toed
  49; ~s 63
pikee 40
pikelet 74
piker 40
pikey 40
pin bone 74
pincer-toed 49
pit 70; ~ of your arm
  41
pitch 89
play 79
plimsoll 80
pod, ~ware 69
pond 70
pool 70
pop 38
pork 66
posh 69
potty 47
pound 36, 70
pour 87
preach 22
prickly-backed
  urchin 62
prickly-pig 62
prickly-urchin 62
pricky-urchin 62
pristine 16
pudding 8
puddled 47
puff 85
puggled 47
pull 8

pullet 8
pulpit 8
pumble-footed 49
pump 80, 85
pup 65; ~py 16, 65
push 8
pusket 69
puss 8
put 8
putt 8

quackle 81
quart 45
queece 63
queest 63
queeze 63
quest 63
quick 19, 45
quiet 45
quist, ~s 63

raddle-head 45
rake 45
rangle 57
regularize 30
riving 45
Romany 40
rooky 47
room 13
rouk 45
ruin 16
rump 66; ~ steak 74
running 23

sandshoe 80
sang 30
sausage 22
scarecrow 46
scared 46
scrod-legged 49
sea-urchin 62
seely 47
set, ~ table, ~ the
  table, ~ the table
  out, ~ the tea; ~ the
  tea out 86
shadow 14
sharp 45
she 32, 34
sheep 11, 12, 36, 66
shell 69; ~ bone 74

shirt 71
shiver 55
shoo (= she) 34
shoot 63, 87, 89
shovel-footed 49
shuck 69
shull 69
shy 89
side 66
sieve 11
silly 47
sin, since 78
sine 78
sing 17, 30
sirloin 66
sister 1
skend 51
skenning 51
skirt 71
slack, ~ coal 74
slag 74
slatch 74
sleaze, sleazy 65
slew 89
sling 89
sliver 55
sly-footed 49
small coal 74
smit, ~e, ~ting, ~tle,
  ~tling 58
smudge 58
smut 58
sneck 42
snicket 79
snitch, ~er 42
snotter 42
snout 42
soak 87
sock 89
soldier 25
soot 7, 13
sorrow 14
sparrow 14; ~-grass
  67
speak 12
speel 55
speld 55
spelk 55
spell 54, 55, 79
spile 55
spill 55

spinach 22
spindle 54
spit 84
splawdered 49
splay-footed 49
splint, ~er 55
spoke 54
spool 55
sprog-hocked 49
squeamish 45
squint, ~-eyed 51
stab, ~ber 54
staff 54
stale 54
stall 54
stap 54
staups 47
stave 54
stavver 54
stay 54
steak bone 74
steak piece 74
stee-spell 54
stee-step 54
steel 11
stell 70
step 54
stifle 81
stoit 80
stone 89
stop 90
stot 80
stower 54
straddly-bandy 49
strangle 81
street 11
stronger 17
strongest 17
stupid 24
sun 3, 6, 7, 8, 9
sung 30
swad, ~dle 69
sward 69
swarth 69
swathe 69
swear, ~ing 83

sweetmeat 12
swimmy, ~-headed
   52
swimy 52
swine 36

tab 42
tabby, ~-cat 60
tag 42
taking 58
tamp 80
teach 88
tear-down 45
teem 79, 87
the 35
thee 33
their, ~n, ~s 35
they 32
thine 35
thirl 53
thistle 21
thock 85
thou 33
thought 21
three 21
throat 81
thropple 81
throttle 81
throw 89
Thursday 24
thwart-eyed 51
thy 35
tib 60
tiff 85
tift 85
timber-toed 49
to 26
token 88
tongue 17
tool 47
tosie 49
toss 89
touched 47
train (= teach) 88
troll-footed 49
trunk 42

tucks 44
Tuesday 24, 25
tun 73
turn 15
turnpike, ~-road-
   sailors, ~-sailors
   40
twang-toed 49
twilly-toed 49
two of 31
two on 31

under your arm 41
under-arm 41
underneath your arm
   41
upstrigolous 45
urchin 62
us 26, 32
us two 31

vim 45
viper 59
virtue 24
vixen 20

waff 85
waken 45
walk, ~ed 30
wallow 53
wander 45
want 8
wappy 47
warch 56
ware 69
wark 56
Warwick 28
way 90
way wo 90
we 11, 32; ~ are 32;
   ~ two 31
weak 11
weal 54
web-footed 49

Wednesday 24;
   ~-and-Thursday
   49
wee 90
wem-footed 49
wet 87
whang 89
wheel 19
whelp 19, 65
when 65
whet 65
which 65
whilst 27
whin 68, 79
whip 19
whirly 52
whoa 90
wick 19, 45
wicker 42
widgeon 16
widow 14
wiggy-arsed 45
wo, ~ back, ~ ho,
   ~ there 90
woa 90
woag 90
woat 90
wolf 8
woman 8, 18
womb 82
wonky 52
wood 8; ~quest 63
wool 8, 18
work 56; ~mate 39
worm 59
wup 90

yap 53
yark 89
ye 33
yea 90
year 18
yellow 14
you 33
youngster 37
your, ~n, ~s 35